MAXIMUM RECOVERY
INSURANCE CLAIMS
DEMYSTIFIED

A 40 year veteran of the industry
clarifies the process

FREDERICK STATEN

iUniverse, Inc.
New York   Bloomington

Maximum Recovery - Insurance Claims Demystified
A 40 year veteran of the industry clarifies the process

iUniverse books may be ordered through booksellers or by contacting:

iUniverse
1663 Liberty Drive
Bloomington, IN 47403
www.iuniverse.com
1-800-Authors (1-800-288-4677)

Because of the dynamic nature of the Internet, any Web addresses or links contained in this
book may have changed since publication and may no longer be valid. The views expressed
in this work are solely those of the author and do not necessarily reflect the views of the
publisher, and the publisher hereby disclaims any responsibility for them.

ISBN: 978-1-4502-3638-6 (pbk)
ISBN: 978-1-4502-3639-3 (ebook)

Printed in the United States of America

iUniverse rev. date: 6/15/10

Preface

Those loud noises you heard, when you opened the cover of this book, were the agonized protests of insurance executives and plaintiffs' lawyers seeing that you are about to acquire information that might threaten their profit margins.

The seed for this work, planted more than fifty years ago in the mountains of Appalachia, grew through a million miles of highways, dusty roads, hillside shacks, hospital corridors, boardrooms and courtrooms. Engraved in memory are a thousand anguished faces, a few pontifical stuffed shirts, and enough greed to encompass a large part of the underworld for all of eternity.

Over a career that spanned more than four decades as a member of the insurance team, the author investigated, settled or supervised thousands of insurance claims of every kind; so while there is no promise that the information presented will lead you to that mythical pot of gold, it will give you an insider's view of the claims process. There is no intent, however for this work to serve as a manual for the presentation of fraudulent or exaggerated claims.

The author is not a lawyer, but has spent his entire adult life rubbing elbows and matching wits with the best and the brightest of them, many of whom may be counted among his closest friends. Most have provided practical knowledge of a noble but much maligned profession, knowledge that transcends that which might have been gained in a classroom.

The average consumer is lost in a bewildering maze of confusion following an accident or insurable casualty loss. An insurance policy, with its exceptions, exclusions, limitations and legal jargon is replete with ambiguous clauses. Most states have enacted legislation to require their readability, yet people still find these contracts about as easy to read and interpret as documents written in ancient Greek. It is the author's purpose here to demystify some of the terms and conditions contained in various policies in addition to providing a detailed explanation of the procedures used by insurance companies to dispose of your claim. We also provide some counter measures to the companies' tactics. Maximum Recovery discloses no deeply guarded secrets of the industry, but here, under a single cover, are all of the facts you will need to pursue your claim in a way that will permit you to receive every dime to which you are entitled as compensation for your injury or damage.

To some extent Maximum Recovery, as the title implies, is in opposition to the efforts of tort reform proponents who would give free rein to the manufacturers of faulty or dangerous products and the negligent providers of professional services. It is that and more. Litigation to resolve disputes and compensate innocent victims of wrongs is an important facet of civilized society because it serves as a deterrent to reckless behavior, corporate chicanery and malpractice in all of the professions.

Reformers often cite abuses in the systems that create sensational damage awards with contingent legal fees that are disproportionate to the efforts of the attorney. Undeniably, these cases happen, but they are rare, and the trial judge or an appellate court often reduces the judgments.

Nothing on the pages that follow intends to incite the presentation of fraudulent or overstated claims, but the information conveyed will fortify you with knowledge that will enable you to receive compensation for injury or damage while eliminating needless expense. By knowing what to expect from insurance companies and attorneys, you will find yourself in a far better position to respond, saving hundreds, if not thousands, of dollars.

In using the masculine pronouns *he and his* throughout this work, each personal reference is equally applicable to either sex. The forms employed are for grammatical simplification and not intended to be sexist.

Table of Contents

Introduction

You never saw the truck as it approached the intersection. Two witnesses, who were standing on the corner, said the driver was using his cell phone as he drove his heavily loaded 18-wheeler through the stop sign. There was an ear splitting crash and the screech of tires as your car careened across the pavement then rolled over at least twice before it came to rest on its top. Torn metal and shattered glass were all around you.

White hot pain enveloped your entire body, and in your semiconscious state, stark terror raced through your mind. The entire event took place in seconds. A little later, there were voices in the background and probing hands reaching through the broken window next to you. Smoke or steam billowed from the smashed engine compartment of your car, and in the distance, you could hear the scream of police and ambulance sirens. In a matter of minutes that seemed like hours, the rescue squad arrived. The paramedics carefully and expertly removed you from the wreckage. They placed a cervical collar on your neck, and lifted you onto a backboard. Another member of the EMT team worked to control the bleeding from a deep laceration in your thigh. The team placed you in an ambulance and while one of the crew administered intravenous fluids, the ambulance sped to the nearest hospital emergency room. The pain subsided into numbness, and for the first time, you noticed that you could not move your legs.

Thus began day one of a long siege of pain, anguish and a struggle to recover from a disaster that took place through no fault of your own. Physical recovery would be prolonged and never complete. In the meantime, your income has ceased and your expenses begin to soar. What happens to your family? Where do you go from here?

No matter who you are or where you are, you may be only the blink of an eye from becoming a player in the foregoing scenario or one like it. If you are a homeowner, a lawyer or a doctor, a victim of an accident, a business owner, insurance adjuster, insurance agent, insurance executive, law student or a potential juror, there is something in this book of value to you. If you or your business has suffered an insured loss of any kind, there is a treasure trove of valuable information within these pages. Before you make that call to the television lawyer who is soliciting you as a client, read further. The knowledge you will gain can save you thousands of dollars.

Because we are sharing our experience with personal injury, property damage and wrongful death claims arising from the fault of others, you should regard this book as a supplement, not as a substitute, for good legal advice. You are dealing with matters that involve adversarial interests and have the potential to wind their way into the world of lawyers--- the civil justice system.

This work will provide you with vital information surrounding the entire spectrum of insurance claims and assist you with making important decisions in the financial recovery process. Topics covered in section I include claims covered under homeowners, automobile, professional and commercial liability policies including injuries, death and damage arising from defective or unreasonably dangerous products. Section II deals with both personal and commercial property losses.

As a result of its superior position with respect to time and financial resources, the advantage will always rest with the insurance company, but with a comprehensive understanding of the process by which claims are handled and settled, you will at least make strides toward a more level playing field.

PART I

Personal Injury And Property Damage Claims

The Claims Recipe

Negligence, Duty and Damage

The first hurdle that must be cleared for the creation of a viable personal injury or property damage claim is proof of partial or total fault on the part of another. It is correct to say that negligent conduct is the triggering mechanism for a claim, but there is more. There must also be injury or damage arising from the act or omission of the wrong doer as well as a duty owed to the victim.

In fact, our entire justice system, both criminal and civil, is derived from mans' inherent duty to his fellow man. In legal terms, the negligent act is known as a tort, and the wrongdoer is called a *tort feasor.* The definition of the word *tort* is a *civil wrong that creates injury or damage for which there is a legal remedy.* We all know that accidents happen, and many of them result in terrible injuries. A lazy or impatient victim leaves his shoelaces untied, trips and falls, breaking his neck. Until some enterprising lawyer persuades a court that the shoe lace manufacturer has a duty to put a warning label on its laces that *untied shoe laces have been known to cause tripping and falling, resulting in serious injury or even death,* there is no one to sue. The fault rests with the victim.

For fault or responsibility to exist there must first be a duty, the degree of care one owes to his fellow man, thus creating the truncated legal definition of ordinary negligence; *"the failure to exercise that degree of care as a reasonably prudent person would use under similar*

3

circumstances." For example, the driver of an automobile or truck has a duty to obey traffic laws, preventing his vehicle from colliding with another to the best of his ability. A homeowner or business owner has a duty to warn guests or invitees of any defect on his or her premises that might cause harm, a slippery floor surface etc. In order to be liable, the property owner must have either actual or constructive notice of the hazardous condition. An example of actual notice could be the direct visualization of a wet and slippery floor surface as is often found around the produce counters in a supermarket. The owner's duty to regularly inspect creates a fact that he should have known about hazards such as the slippery floor, inadequate lighting or objects carelessly left in areas that are open to the public. Even if they have not been physically observed by management, it may be shown that with proper inspection, they should have known. This is *constructive notice.*

The manufacturer of a product has a duty to be certain that the product does not contain a defect that makes it unreasonably dangerous for its intended use by its user.

All personal injury and property damage liability is based upon the law of duty, due care and negligence. In some cases such as premises accidents, social guests, business invitees (customers) and licensees, the degree of duty varies with respect to the status of the victim at the time of his injury. Passengers on public conveyances such as aircraft, trains and busses are owed the highest degree of care. Drivers of vehicles have a duty to obey traffic laws and exercise caution to avoid injury and damage to others. Theoretically, business invitees must be shown a higher degree of care than social guests or mere licensees, persons who are given unrestricted access to premises without specific permission. The only duty owed to a trespasser is the avoidance of willful harm. A property owner is prohibited from inflicting injury or damage to the person or property of a person who enters upon the property without permission but poses no threat to the property or its occupants.

You, as the plaintiff, must bear the burden of proof when you sue the party or parties who caused your injuries or damage. You must be able to prove through a preponderance of evidence that the accusations made in your lawsuit are true. If the probability that these allegations are more than 50% likely to be correct, the court must accept them as truth. The defendant has no obligation to prove anything under most circumstances, but may avoid responsibility by disproving your allegations.

During the last half of the twentieth century, there was a major transformation in the civil justice system that has radically altered the way in which legal responsibility is determined. Prior to this revolutionary change, the legal doctrine known as contributory negligence on the part of a victim was, in most states, an absolute bar to recovery against a defendant even though such a defendant was proven to be principally at fault. If the actions of the victim contributed in the slightest way to his injury or damage, then he or she was denied compensation. While this was the law in most jurisdictions, it was seldom strictly applied by the courts or juries. In fact, adjusters and insurance companies usually asserted this argument simply as a talking point in settlement negotiations.

With the gradual erosion of this archaic doctrine, most states have substituted comparative negligence statutes, which impose legal liability on the party who is most responsible for the event, reducing the victim's compensation by his or her percentage of fault but not barring recovery entirely. For the most part, these statutes require that a defendant's negligence constitute more than 49 % of the fault before liability is imposed. The responsibility for allocating the percentage of responsibility is a question for the jury in cases that go to trial. Obviously, a pedestrian has a duty to use caution while crossing a street; so if he fails to look and is then struck by an approaching car, he must bear a part of the blame for the accident. In most states, driving while impaired by alcohol or drugs is negligence as a matter of law, and there is no question that an intoxicated driver is accountable for his or her actions, probably offsetting any moderate negligence on the part of the victim in its entirety.

A recent case from a Manhattan court illustrates the comparative negligence doctrine applied in its extreme circumstances.

An intoxicated man fell from a subway platform in front of an oncoming NYC transit train. The train ran over him, severing his right leg. The jury found that the operator of the subway train would have had time to stop, but did not and was, therefore, principally responsible for the accident. They awarded $3,594,943 to the injured man, but since a jury decided that he was 35% responsible for the accident, the award was reduced correspondingly to $2,336,713. This case also demonstrates the principle that no one can predict the decision a jury will reach in any given set of circumstances.

Another recently reported case involved an eight-year-old boy who fell from a jungle gym located on the premises of a Burger King Restaurant in Temecula, California. The boy, Jacob Buckett, accompanied by his father and younger sister, were patrons of the restaurant when the boy attempted to climb on the gym, lost his grip and fell. He struck his head on the tile floor, suffered serious brain damage and was in a coma for two months. The child's parents contended that both Burger King and the franchise owner were aware of the dangerous condition because of previous accidents. Extensive brain damage left the boy with permanent impairment to the extent that his maturity level is less than half that of his current age of 12. Burger King has recently settled the case for the sum of $20,000,000.

A chart showing the type of comparative negligence rule for each of the 50 states is contained in appendix II.

All of the injuries and property damage arising from this multitude of circumstances fall potentially within some form of personal or commercial liability insurance. Known as third party coverage, it provides a source of restitution, which might not otherwise be available from the wrongdoer

Considering the widespread acceptance of the comparative negligence doctrine, it is obvious that insurance adjusters will make a strenuous effort to attribute a percentage of responsibility for an accident to the victim.

In order for a claim to survive against a responsible party or parties there must first be a recognizable tort. This act or omission is termed a cause of action.

Listed here are some of many common sources of injury and financial loss.

- *Failure to provide the standard of care required of the involved profession.*
- *Injury or death resulting from use of a defective or unreasonably dangerous product.*
- *Death or injuries resulting from common carrier accidents such as those involving airplanes, buses, trains, even taxi cabs.*
- *Injuries from dog bites or other animal attacks.*
- *Injury to reputation as a result of libel, slander or defamation of character.*
- *Injuries and damage caused by the intentional acts of others.*
- *Injury or death from any negligent act of another in which the probability of injury H Injury or death resulting from negligent operation of car, truck or motorcycle.*
- *Tripping, slipping and falling due to a concealed hazard.*

Product Liability

Liability for a defective product that is proven to cause injury can extend to the manufacturer, distributor or seller of the product. Unlike cases that arise from ordinary negligence, it is usually not necessary for a victim to prove negligence on the part of a defendant, only that the product, when used for its intended purpose, was defective or unreasonably dangerous. Like most of our civil justice laws, the underlying legal theory supporting this doctrine goes back to the English common law. Originally, the law held that there must be a relationship between a victim and the seller or manufacturer known as privity before an injured party could sue. This limited personal injury actions to purchasers in the sales transaction. This is no longer true. Any person who suffers injury or damage resulting from the use of a defective or dangerous product may sue the manufacturer, the distributor, the retail seller or anyone who participated in placing the product in the stream of commerce.

One important case that eventually resulted in a massive class action lawsuit was against the manufacturer of an insulation material that was used in farm buildings such as horse barns and chicken brooder houses. When exposed to a source of ignition, the material was highly flammable and acted as an accelerant. Numerous fires that resulted from a variety of ignition sources were much more destructive due to the inflammability of this product.

In addition to a count of strict liability, a victim may include additional counts for negligence and breach of warranty, both express and implied. If it can be proven that a manufacturer knew that its product was defective or unreasonably dangerous to the consumer, yet continued with its production and sale; then the injured party might include a count of negligence, subjecting the manufacturer to a potential assessment of punitive damages.

One of the most widely publicized product liability claims was the case of Liebeck V. McDonald's Restaurants.

There was outrage on the part of the media and many citizens who cited this case to illustrate the frivolous nature of suits under our civil justice system. But the media coverage did not include most of the facts concerning Liebeck's in juries.

Stella Liebeck, a 79 year old woman from Albuquerque, New Mexico purchased a cup of coffee at a McDonald's drive in window while she was seated in the passenger seat of her car driven by her grandson. The grandson parked the car and Mrs. Liebeck placed the cup of coffee between her knees. In attempting to remove the lid to add cream and sugar, she spilled the entire cup of coffee on her lap. Evidence showed that McDonalds has made a practice of serving coffee at 180-190 *F which is a scalding temperature, capable of causing third degree burns in a matter of seconds. The plaintiff, Liebeck, did, in fact, suffer third degree burns, was hospitalized for eight days, underwent skin grafting and her treatment continued for two years.

Liebeck's attorney sued McDonalds on the theory that the corporation was guility of gross negligence for serving coffee that was "unreasonably dangerous." Settlement efforts failed, and the case went to trial. The jury concluded that under the comparative negligence doctrine, McDonald's was 80% responsible for the plaintiff's injuries and the plaintiff, herself, was 20% responsible. The original verdict was in amount of $200,000 for compensatory damages and $2.7 million in punitive damages. The court reduced the verdict to a combined total in amount of $640,000.

McDonald's appealed, and before a decision was reached on the appeal, the case was settled for an undisclosed amount. McDonalds, as you may have noticed, no longer serves coffee at a scalding temperature.

In the accident that was described in the introduction to this book, you will recall that the innocent driver's vehicle upset after it was "T-boned" in the intersection. Assuming that it was one of the sport utility vehicles that have been shown to be unstable and susceptible to overturning in these situations, then it is possible that the victim would have a cause of action against the automobile manufacturer as well as the offending truck driver. In addition to proving the design defect, the injured party would also have to prove that some or all of his injuries would not have occurred but for the upset.

The strict liability doctrine can be applied to other injury cases such as those that are inflicted by wild animals owned by the wrongdoer and from activities that are known to be extra hazardous such as the use of explosives or other dangerous materials.

Litigation in these matters is complex; requiring special expertise on the part of both plaintiffs' and defense attorneys. Provisions of the law vary from one state to another, and the judicial decisions that establish legal precedent in products liability are too numerous to calculate. The foregoing summary is the bare tip of a huge iceberg. If you have been injured or suffered serious damage resulting from the use of any product, or inherently dangerous activity, you need to find an attorney who has been successful in the prosecution of these cases.

Liquor Liability

There are thousands of alcohol related accidents every year, and there is little question that the intoxicated wrong doer is legally liable for his outrageously negligent conduct. Responsibility for injuries resulting from these accidents may also impose liability on the establishment that served the beer, wine or liquor that caused the wrongdoer's intoxication. In most states, a bartender has a duty to withhold additional drinks to a person who is clearly intoxicated or is known to have consumed enough alcohol that would be likely to induce intoxication. For example, consider the following illustration; a scenario that occurs with great regularity.

Wally and his foursome have just finished their 18 hole round at the local club. They are, as is their custom, sitting in the bar having a few cold ones and paying off their bets to the winners. Wally is not a beer drinker, but prefers to indulge in a very dry martini. The bartender is noted for his extreme generosity in his mixed drink preparation; so Wally's martinis are not only extra dry, they are extra large. The group lingers a little longer than usual, and it is likely that none of them could pass a blood alcohol test, especially Wally, who by this time has had several refills that were essentially straight gin. His eyes had begun to droop and by the time it came to have "one more for the road," his speech was slurred.

As he drove off the parking lot in his new Mercedes, Wally was barely awake but accustomed to this routine, he was confident in his ability to make his way safely home.

It was dark by the time he was half way home, the combination of fatigue from his round of golf and a near drunken stupor from alcohol consumption overwhelmed him, and he dozed off, never to reawaken. His car went out of control into oncoming traffic in the opposing lane. The head on crash was with a sport utility vehicle driven by a woman and accompanied by her two children. Wally and all three occupants of the SUV were pronounced dead at the scene. The medical examiner's investigation, following the accident, disclosed that Wally's blood alcohol level was more than twice the legal limit.

Wally's insurance company, his personal estate, the country club that purveyed the alcohol and, if the club had one, their liquor liability insurers were all in a world of trouble. What jury would not award enormous damages in a case such as this?

Liquor liability is covered under Dram Shop Acts, laws which have been established by a majority of states that impose liability on commercial establishments for the irresponsible sale of alcohol. There is substantial diversity in these laws. Some include responsibility for injuries sustained by the establishment's patron while others do not. There are states that impose liability on social hosts, but most do not.

If your injury results from the actions of a drunken driver or the operator of any other conveyance, and it can be proven that the accident would not have occurred but for the wrongdoer's intoxication, you or your attorney should explore the issue of liquor liability.

Professional Liability and Other Interpersonal Relationships

Many accidents and injuries result from the negligent conduct of neighbors, friends and relatives, family doctors and other professionals. In these circumstances, there may be reluctance on your part to initiate legal action against people with whom you have a close personal relationship, but this should not prevent the assertion of your legal rights if you suffer a serious injury. Most people will be sympathetic to your cause; although they must use caution to avoid any appearance of collusion with you in the prosecution of your claim. The wrong doer has a duty under his insurance coverage to cooperate in defending your claim, and failure to do so could result in denial of coverage. Logically though, who would suspect your friend or relative to show more bias to the insurance company's interest than he does to yours.

As soon as possible after the accident, you should have a frank discussion with the responsible party concerning the basis for your claim and ask that a report be made to the appropriate insurance company, (auto, homeowners, etc.); depending upon where and how the accident occurred. If the facts are undisputed, there should be no reason for a rancorous confrontation between you and the wrong doer. You can explain that you understand there was no intent to cause you harm, but you are entitled to compensation. Point out that you will make every effort to settle with the insurance company and avoid litigation, but if a lawsuit becomes necessary, no personal recrimination is intended.

Reluctance to make a claim for malpractice against a trusted physician who has treated you and your family for years is understandable. Unless the practitioner has clearly committed outrageous negligence that caused you serious harm, then the claim should not be pursued. Doctors cannot guarantee that the treatment they render will produce a successful result, and it is highly unlikely that any person who offers professional service will have a totally unblemished career. Simple mistakes occur, but they do not all constitute negligence that justifies the filing of a malpractice lawsuit. Think long and hard before you bring a case against your doctor or other health care professional. On the other hand, if a physician or other health care provider's practice falls clearly below the standard of care for his or her specialty, then you probably should proceed. Defining *standard of care* requires expert review of the facts.

One of the reasons for the plethora of lawsuits for medical malpractice can be attributed to a self-righteous attitude on the part of many physicians. Unlike other forms of liability insurance, the medical malpractice policy contains a provision requiring the insured physician's *consent to settle*. No doctor wants a blemished record, and many are unwilling to accept responsibility for the act or omission that forms the basis for a patient's complaint. By declining an opportunity for settlement, they, consequently, leave the patient no alternative to litigation.

Damages

The Value of your Claim

The amount that your claim is worth in settlement depends upon many things, but in the final analysis, it is you, your attorney and the insurance company's best judgment as to the amount you might be awarded by a jury of your peers. Any sum less than that plus the insurance company's cost of defense would be attractive to the insurance company, but the controversy arises from the divergence of opinion between the three interested parties. You can bet that the dollar amount that you and your attorney have in mind will be much greater than the insurance carrier's evaluation.

There is no uniformity to jury verdicts. The only thing about which they are predictable is that they are unpredictable. No one can tell you precisely what six to twelve of your peers will decide after hearing your case, no matter how well it is presented. Juries represent a cross section of the adult population, ranging through the entire spectrum of human intelligence. Some people are frugal to the extreme. Others are blind to the true value of money. Many have great difficulty understanding the law of negligence and the determination of legal liability. Some mistakenly believe that fault depends upon the intentional act of a perpetrator. There is a tendency on the part of juries in rural areas to be more conservative or less generous with their verdicts than juries in large metropolitan areas are. Verdicts rendered against individuals are likely to be smaller than those against corporations are. Sex, age and racial ethnicity of the victim are also components that play a role in the size of verdicts. The truth is that almost no jury is qualified to render a flawless decision in any complicated lawsuit. For these and many other reasons, settlement is preferable to a jury trial for both parties.

Some companies have made it a practice to settle any case in which the outcome depends upon a jury's interpretation of the evidence. Going to trial is an option reserved only for those cases in which a successful defense based upon a rule of law is a reasonable expectation.

The insurance industry, its lobbyists, political friends and business interests have made a concerted effort to curtail litigation in personal injury cases, and to a very large extent, this effort has been supported by political administrations on both the national and state levels. Awards for general damages such as pain and suffering have been eliminated or drastically reduced in several states through tort reform legislation.

The only remedy offered by our system of justice for personal injury is money. Is it possible to calculate the reasonable dollar amount for a lifetime of pain caused by a wrongfully inflicted injury? The cost of pain management using a medical specialist is possible to calculate, but the ongoing suffering bears no relationship to dollars and cents. If the pain causes a limitation in the victim's physical activity, it is certain to have a detrimental effect on his general health over the long term. These are factors demanding serious consideration in settlement negotiations or the deliberations of a jury. The truth is that the money damages for imponderables such as pain and suffering or the loss of the normal enjoyment of life will be the amount the jury decides to award.

To gain public support for elimination or reduction of these awards, there has been wide publicity circulated to promote the industry's position that the cost of litigation is ultimately passed on to the consumer through the increased cost of insurance and other products. There could be a fragment of truth to this argument, but it is meaningless to the victim seeking fair compensation for injuries and damage. Bear in mind that amounts paid in claims is but one element in the complicated process of ratemaking. Executive compensation, advertising and marketing expenses play substantial roles.

For some time now, major companies have employed the results of a computerized system called *Colossus* that assists with claims evaluation through a comprehensive statistical process. The program attempts to forecast the probable amount of a jury verdict based upon what has taken place in similar cases in the past. It seems unlikely that a program of this kind, regardless of sophistication, can read the minds of potential jurors who are the ultimate deciders of fact, but despite the question of its reliability, this system is still employed by many companies for making settlement decisions or initial offers.

Some companies evaluate claims based upon a multiple of the victim's out of pocket expenses. For example, two or two and one half times the medical and hospital bills, lost wages and property damage. It is not a very scientific approach to compensating the injured victim, but it works for many companies. If you are led to believe that you will earn such a large multiple of your out of pocket expenses in your final settlement, would you or would you not be tempted to prolong your return to work and unnecessarily increase your other expenses?

The term damage, as used in the legal sense, refers to loss or injury caused by the negligent act of another. It includes, loss of present and future income, cost of medical care, nursing or domestic services, permanent injury, pain and suffering, including mental anguish and all of the elements that constitute damages for which a victim is entitled to be compensated in the legal process.

In addition to individual damages, there may be, in the case of a married victim, a separate cause of action by the victim's spouse for *loss of consortium*. This includes deprivation of the conjugal relationship and companionship as well as other intangibles and services that exist between husband and wife. It will be interesting to see how the courts deal with cases in states that have given legal sanction to same sex marriage and the rights of the significant other in this age of extra marital cohabitation. Where unions of this kind have been granted legal standing, there is no reason to believe that they will be treated differently than the traditional married male and female couple. It would seem that all the benefits that accrue to the surviving spouse in a wrongful death case would be similarly available to the surviving partner in a same sex commitment. If such cases have not already been presented for a decision by the courts, you can be assured that they will be forthcoming in the near future. Sexual bias will obviously play a role in the jury's decision to award damages in these circumstances especially for the loss of a sexual relationship.

The term *damages* refer to amounts of money awarded for any and all of the above. In cases involving egregious negligence by the wrong doer, the court may also assess punitive damages. For example, if the manufacturer of a product containing a defect that is known to cause death or serious injury continues to manufacture and distribute the product just to reduce production costs, the company would, if sued, likely subject itself to a punitive damage award. Since punitive damages are almost always excluded in liability insurance coverage, this legal standard has imposed severe restrictions on the manufacturers and distributors of almost all products, especially automobiles, aircraft and their components.

As soon as a lawsuit is filed against its insured, the insurer is confronted with the burden of defense costs. Unless the company involved uses house counsel to defend these cases, then the meter begins to run in the office of their outside defense firm the minute the case is assigned. Every activity that takes place represents an hourly charge for the firm's services. Every telephone call, memo, conference, pleading, response to motions, the filing of interrogatories, depositions of witnesses and a myriad of other activities rapidly accumulate before the trial begins. In very serious cases, more than one attorney often represents the insurer. Billed at a rate of several hundred dollars per hour, the expense incurred for the defense of a lawsuit becomes a major factor in the decision to defend or settle.

In the final analysis, the value of your claim depends largely on your injuries and your provable economic losses. But even if you have a claim that might produce a multi-million dollar verdict, its final value is the amount that can be recovered from the wrongdoer's assets or insurance limits. If the responsible entity is a large corporation or an agency of government, then the potential for a settlement at or near its true value increases exponentially.

In some high exposure cases, companies may attempt to settle for less than their policy limit; however they will not pursue this effort with much diligence because it can subject them to a judgment beyond their policy limit. Remember, insurance companies must respond to claims in a manner that will protect their policyholders, not themselves.

Catastrophic Injuries

Certain injuries are of such a devastating nature that they have lifelong implications and are tragically catastrophic. They include closed head injuries with brain damage, burns over a large part of the body, amputation of one or more limbs, loss of vision and spinal cord injuries that result in complete or partial paralysis.Injuries in this class invariably create multiple victims especially if the injured party needs to rely upon a family member or members for his care and support. In the case of persons who have no family support, they simply become wards of the state.

Money will not restore a severed limb, heal a damaged spinal cord or arouse a comatose patient who suffers from brain damage, but following recovery from life threatening conditions, many of these victims will continue to live long, potentially tortured lives. Those who have access to necessary financial resources will fare light years ahead of the less fortunate. The frustration of attempting to obtain the necessary services, adaptations and materials for everyday living by the indigent handicapped is overwhelming. While it has no healing power, money can make the difference between moderate comfort and a life of misery for these people. Assuming that the wrong doer has sufficient assets, any one of these injuries has the potential to generate a multi million-dollar recovery. Yet, disregarding the tremendous cost of caring for these individuals, insurance and tort reform groups offer no exception for them in their misguided efforts to place strict limits on civil damage awards.

The Social Security disability program offers modest assistance; however, it is replete with bureaucratic impediments such as the imposition of strict limitations on the earnings of those who are able to work while disabled. The current limit is less than $1,000. per month. Earnings in excess of the limit result in the cessation of disability payments and, even worse, the termination of Medicare coverage.

Even though some of these people, with heroic effort, are able to handle limited employment, their disability causes their cost of living to be greater than that of the average able bodied employee, and the ability for them to acquire medical insurance is virtually non existent. These iron clad rules in the Social Security disability program that deal with working while disabled demand some thoughtful and drastic revision.

Most of the well-known charitable institutions, for which fund raisers are especially active and visible, make substantial contributions toward research for the treatment of these injuries, but you must look long and hard to find any services that they provide for individuals. Some state governments are stronger than others in providing assistance for housing, necessary attendant care and medical programs, but faced with increasing deficits and tax revolts, the level of assistance continues to shrink. Sadly, our society seems content to cast these poor wretches on the garbage heap of humanity and ignore them. If called upon to serve on a jury involving one of these cases, you might wish to keep these facts in mind.

Wrongful Death Claims

Every state has a wrongful death statute, which provides for a suit on behalf of the deceased person's beneficiaries such as parent, spouse or children against the person who caused the death of the father, mother, child or spouse. In addition to compensatory damages for the loss of the deceased, some states also permit a jury to include an award for conscious pain and suffering by the deceased before he or she expired.

In some jurisdictions, a jury may award damages to the decedent's personal representative or next of kin simply for the loss of life or the enjoyment of life. As in personal injury cases, there may also be an award to the spouse of the decedent for loss of companionship, conjugal relations and other services common to marital relations as well as mental anguish.

Prior to the enactment of these statutes, there was no cause of action for wrongful death. Under the common law, it was the theory that the claims expired upon the death of the decedent. Unless the statute provides for emotional damages, the lives of minor children have little value. The cost to rear and educate them constitute liabilities rather than assets, but in states where emotional damages are recognized, substantial awards can be made for the wrongful death of a minor child.

To prove pecuniary loss from the death of a spouse or parent, it is necessary to establish the decedent's normal life expectancy and a projection of income for the remainder of his or her life. This involves computation of the future value of money, anticipation of increased earnings and many other factors. The skilled plaintiffs' attorney in these cases will call upon the services of an economist as an expert witness to testify concerning this element of damages.

As in almost all-personal injury litigation, if the wrongdoer's negligence in causing the accident is flagrant, such as driving under the influence of alcohol or drugs, then a jury is more likely to render a higher monetary judgment.

The complexity of these case almost always require the employment of an attorney. As a layman, you are not qualified to address the nuances surrounding a wrongful death claim. The attorney will represent you on a contingent fee basis. You will pay nothing unless there is a recovery on your behalf. Do not hesitate to engage in some bargaining for a reduction in the usual 25% to 50% of the amount recovered. Also be aware that the statute of limitations in a wrongful death lawsuit may not be the same as the personal injury statute.

Personal Injury and Property Damage Checklist

1. Get the best medical attention available.
2. Investigate the circumstances of the accident.
3. Thoroughly document your injuries and damages. Get help from a family member or friend. If none are available, consider hiring a professional accident reconstruction specialist and a commercial photographer
4. If you or your representative are able to speak with the wrong doer, try to get complete insurance information, especially the policy limits and the responsible party's net worth.
5. Seek out temporary financial assistance, i.e., Social Security Disability, workers' compensation, health insurance, accidental disability insurance and your own auto policy.
6. Speak with the adjuster, but sign nothing and be cautious in discussing the accident, your injuries, and your personal financial circumstances.
7. If your claim arises out of an automobile accident, be sure to give prompt notice to your own insurance carrier. Be aware of the coverage provided by uninsured or underinsured motorist coverage. If your policy includes medical payments coverage, use it to pay some or all of your medical expenses.
8. Be aware of the time period that limits the time for filing suit.
9. If your injuries will result in serious permanent disability, a shortened life expectancy or the death of a loved one, *hire an attorney*. Bear in mind that this is the most important step of all your post injury activities. Carefully consider the criteria set forth in *Hiring an Attorney*. Do not sign the retainer agreement until you have negotiated the fee.

10. If you are offered a structured settlement based upon an annuity purchased from a life insurance company, weigh its benefits in comparison to a lump sum. Be certain that the life insurance company has the highest financial rating.

11. If you are compelled to submit to a physical examination by a physician design-nated by the defendant's insurance company, be sure that you or your attorney are furnished with a copy of the physician's report and keep a record of the time actually spent in the examination.

12. When you go to trial, look your best. Dress conservatively, avoid any emotional outbreaks or gestures, answer questions clearly but do not elaborate unnecessarily.

Insurance Companies and Their Products

Insurance is a contractual arrangement in which companies calculate risks; attempt to predict the long-term costs of claims and other expenses then collect premiums based upon these calculations in the sale of their contracts. Actuarial specialists, based on historical experience, current trends and, to some extent, guesswork, generally make these predictions. The premium dollar covers operating expenses, taxes and claims. If this distribution is less than 100%, then the balance represents underwriting profit. In the meantime, premiums collected are invested to produce additional income and surplus growth. The industry relies heavily on investment income and diversification to create a positive bottom line, but the requirements for careful underwriting and claims practices are still priorities with all companies. Stock companies operate for the benefit of their shareholders.

Their policyholders own mutual insurance companies and the ideal reason for their existence is to provide standard insurance at the lowest possible cost. With tongue in cheek; however, many executives of these companies admit that mutual companies exist for the benefit of their officers, directors and agents. There is no obvious distinction between stock and mutual companies with respect to claims practices.

Numerous complex procedures are not spelled out here. Due to the scope of this work, the foregoing is merely an outline of a company's financial operations. Giant companies are really conglomerates with a vast array of financial interests throughout the world. One such company has been a featured player in recent news events concerning its near fatal involvement in the mortgage derivative scandal. If it had collapsed, hundreds of thousands of claims would have gone unpaid creating a domino effect throughout the insurance industry. With its payment of huge bonuses to its executive force, this huge company remains an object of intense controversy.

With the pressure placed upon state regulators by their lobbyists, insurers have successfully refused to include profits from investments in their bottom line results for the purpose of rate making, but the investment of premium income is as much a part of the business as underwriting and probably should be included as a factor in the rate making Even loss reserves, sums set aside for the payment of claims, continue to produce investment income until claims are actually paid, but never the less, specialized insurance accounting permits the use of these reserves to offset profits. From this you can see that time is always on the side of the insurance company. The longer it can keep your money, the more it will earn.

Insurance products come in a seemingly endless variety of forms, written by hundreds of companies. Black's Law Dictionary devotes almost five pages to the definition of the word insurance. There are property policies, liability policies, life and health policies and many others, but they all have one thing in common. Policies are contracts in which the insurance company promises, in exchange for a premium, to compensate those it insures for losses and claims arising from specific contingencies. These contracts are called contracts of adhesion, so called because their terms and provisions are not subject to bargain or negotiation by the consumer. They are simply forms prepared by the insurance company and offered on a take it or leave it basis. Like most other contracts, any ambiguities and contradictory clauses are construed against the preparer.

The industry is subject to regulation and licensing through the states in which it operates. Companies are required to file their rates and policy forms with state insurance departments for approval, and the terms and conditions of a company's policies must conform to the law in the state where they are written. Most states have also adopted regulations that prohibit unfair or deceptive acts as set forth in the Unfair Trade Practices Model Act created by the National Association of Insurance Commissioners. For examples of the prohibited activities, an overview of the model act is included as appendix II.

The degree to which these rules are enforced depends on the state in which the grievance occurs. Most of the state commissioners are either political appointees or elected officials. They are the target of intense lobbying by the insurance industry with the result that their rulings often favor the industry and not the consumer. At this time, there is no Federal regulation of the insurance industry because of the McCarran-Ferguson Act, legislation that enacted in the 1940s to exempt the industry from the Commerce Clause. The act does not necessarily prevent the Federal government from enacting regulatory laws, but, up to now, it has continued to extend broad authority for such regulation to the states. It remains to be seen, how this will play out in the new health care reform efforts in the current political administration.

Without insurance, our economy would probably collapse, a fact that is apparent from the troubled world of coverage for product liability. The frequency and severity of claims arising from manufacturing defects has made the cost of liability insurance for some products almost prohibitive, causing some well-known companies to cease production and making start ups of new and innovative products extremely expensive. For several years, the production of light aircraft and their engines ceased. Some automobiles and other products, such as prescription drugs, were removed from the market. This brought about a frantic clamor from conservative politicians for the enactment of tort reform, eliminating or limiting your ability to sue a wrong doer for the injuries and damages that you sustain. There is no doubt that these efforts originated with lobbyists from the insurance industry and major corporations. They are among the most powerful "Special interest groups.", and it is *their ox that is being gored.*

Liability Insurance

Liability insurance coverage is designed to protect the insured person, business or professional enterprise from claims made against them by others for which they may be legally responsible

The liability coverage of a package policy such as the Homeowners, automobile and commercial multi-peril is found in Section II of these contracts where all of the terms, conditions and exclusions are described. Section I deals with coverage for damage to or destruction of the property insured such as buildings and personal property owned by the insured or, in the case of automobile insurance, the car itself.

In liability insurance parlance, the party who is making claim for personal injury or property damage is the claimant. The person from whom the claimant is seeking compensation is the defendant, the responsible party or from the standpoint of the insurance company, the insured. The victim should understand that his claim is against the person who caused his injury or damage, not the insurance company who represents that individual, corporation or more than one person. The insurance company has agreed that it will settle or defend claims made against its insured, but in almost all states the company cannot be named as a party to the victim's lawsuit. In fact, the disclosure of insurance to a jury can often be grounds for a mistrial. This is based upon the theory that knowledge of insurance by the jury could diminish their ability to render an impartial verdict.

The insuring agreement of a liability insurance policy states that it will pay or defend the insured for all claims caused by accident or occurrence for which the insured may become legally liable. There is a limit of liability contained in the declarations page of the policy. This limit sets forth the maximum the company will pay for personal injury or property damage. In an automobile policy, this is usually written in a split form, such as $100,000 Per person, $200,000 Per accident and $50,000 For property damage. The amounts stated here are for illustration only. They can be more or less, depending on the choice of the insured party and some policies are sold with a single limit, covering all three contingencies. Over and above this limit, the company agrees to bear the expense to defend suits arising from accidents where the insured may be legally liable. So, in responding to your claim either before or after suit is filed, the insurance company is simply acting on behalf of its insured to which it owes a contractual duty. If the limit of liability set forth in the policy is not sufficient to cover a verdict rendered against the insured, then the victim can still proceed against the personal assets of that party or parties.

This imposes some special duties on the insurance carrier where its negligent or deliberate failure to perform can result in the extension of its coverage to pay amounts above the limits set forth in the policy. For example, if it can be shown that the insurer had an opportunity to settle within the limits of its policy but negligently failed to do so, this can create the possibility of what is known as an excess judgment, an order by the court that the insurance carrier must pay the entire claim, regardless of its limit. There are often situations in which the insured defendant also has coverage under a separate policy called an umbrella liability policy. This policy usually will provide a much higher limit than the underlying coverage. This coverage only becomes operative after the underlying limit is exhausted. If, during the ongoing settlement negotiations before trial, the umbrella carrier believes that the claim will exceed the underlying carriers limit it will likely consult with the primary carrier to influence settlement and avoid an exposure of its own limits.

With respect to the coverage for the cost of defense, the company selects, hires and pays the defense attorney. This aspect of the coverage is not subject to a monetary limit until the underlying limits are exhausted. In spite of the fact that the company pays for the defense, the client to whom the attorney owes responsibility is the insured defendant.

It is considered bad faith for an insurance company to place its own interests above those of its insured. If the attorney believes or has reason to believe there is a possibility of a verdict in excess of the policy limit, he is obliged to advise both the company and its insured. In these circumstances, the insured must be afforded an opportunity to have his personal attorney participate in the defense, and some courts have ruled that the insurer is obligated to pay the personal attorney's fees.

In addition to limits of liability, the policy also contains exclusions and conditions that eliminate coverage under certain circumstances. Any act, for example, that is intended from the standpoint of the insured to cause injury or property damage is usually excluded. The question of intent often gives rise to questions as to an insured's actions.

Most of the information thus far has applied to the automobile accident that was described in the introduction to this book. Responsibility was clear and absolute, the injuries incurred were severe and there was strong likelihood of substantial assets with which to pay the claim. Real life situations are seldom that cut and dried. Accidental injuries come in many shades of grey, and, obviously, they do not all arise from automobile accidents. Objects or slippery substances left on floors in public places cause victims to slip, trip and fall. Doctors, nurses and other professionals negligently fail to render treatment in conformity to the standards of their profession. Engineers and contractors make mistakes that result in tragedy. The variety of traumatic incidents that are caused by others on a daily basis are virtually innumerable.

Business owners, landlords, manufacturers and public institutions have a wide array of protection that can be tailored to their needs. These coverages are usually contained within the commercial package policy and include coverage forms for accidents arising from premises, operations and products. These forms may or may not include coverage for completed operations. For example, a contractor finishes a construction project and abandons the job site. The contractor is afforded some limited protection for long term exposure by a law known as a *statute of repose*. This law imposes a date certain after which the filing of a claim against the contractor is barred. The statute of limitations that would normally commence at the time of injury or discovery of an injury is no longer applicable to the contractor's negligent performance; however you might still be able to maintain a case against the property owner who knowingly permits a dangerous condition to exist.

Automobile No Fault Insurance

As of this writing, twelve of the United States plus the District of Columbia have enacted some form of No Fault Insurance Law. The laws vary from one jurisdiction to another; however they all provide for reimbursement to the victim for a percentage of medical expenses, lost wages and loss of services, usually up to $10,000 under the victims own policy without the necessity for litigation against an *at fault* driver.

These statutes prohibit lawsuits unless the victim's injuries reach a certain threshold. Some states impose a monetary threshold while others employ a verbal one. In states that have enacted verbal thresholds, some require that an injured person's disability must exceed a certain number of days or the victim has suffered a permanent injury. To circumvent this restrictive law, many plaintiffs' attorneys have established relationships with friendly chiropractors and physicians who are more liberal and adept at finding permanent disability than others. These statutes were enacted under pressure from the insurance lobby to curtail litigation, but they are woefully inadequate to compensate the injured victim, providing no compensation for pain and suffering or other general damages. It also appears that they have done little to reduce the cost of automobile insurance. Since application of these laws can be circuitous and unwieldy, the injured claimant should consult his attorney in regards to them at the outset.

The states that have enacted No Fault statutes to date are Florida, Hawaii, Kansas, Kentucky, Massachusetts, Michigan, Minnesota, New Jersey, New York, North Dakota, Pennsylvania, and Utah.

Umbrella Liability Insurance

This coverage can be purchased to supplement the underlying limits of a family automobile or homeowners policy. It is a single limit coverage, with a available coverage limits from $1,000,000 to $5,000,000 or more. As its name suggests, the policy provides protection for the insured for those claims that exceed the coverage afforded by the homeowners or automobile policy. These policies are written with a high deductible, and the company will require the insured to purchase limits in the underlying homeowners and auto policies at least equal to the deductible.

Consumers in the upper income brackets, those who have accumulated more assets to protect, most often purchase umbrella policies but this is not always true and the victim of a serious accident should make a strenuous effort to determine whether the wrongdoer has this additional coverage.

Uninsured and Underinsured Motorist Coverage

Uninsured motorist coverage in your own family auto policy typically provides limits equal to the liability limits that you carry; so if the other party had no insurance or not enough to cover your damages, then your own policy would respond. This creates a strong argument in favor of increasing the limits of your own family auto policy to a level as high as you can afford. A reference to the chart in appendix III showing the required automobile liability insurance limits for each state underscores the importance of this coverage. There is a high degree of probability that the person who caused your injury will not have sufficient coverage to satisfy your claim.

If the responsible party has unencumbered assets, the unpaid balance of any judgment over the insurance limit could be collected from those assets such as a home, bank accounts, stocks and bonds or other property of value. As a practical matter, however, most people are often able to hide or shield their personal wealth, if any exists, from judgments. Also, the insurer who provides your uninsured motorist coverage is entitled to reimbursement from the responsible party's assets or estate before you receive any additional payment. Uninsured motorist coverage contains a vast array of exclusions and limitations that require careful study.

Claims Investigation

When an insurer receives an accident report under one of its policies, it will conduct a comprehensive investigation to develop facts that will form the basis for a decision to pay or deny a claim. Initially, the claim is referred to a manager or supervisor who will make a preliminary assessment of it importance and then assign it to an appropriate adjuster for further handling.

The first step in the investigation will be a determination of coverage. Did the accident occur between the inception and expiration dates of the policy period? Does the policy cover the person who is the alleged "wrong doer?" Do the facts reported in the initial report fall within the scope of coverage? Are there any applicable exclusions that might preclude coverage? Has the insured party made any material misrepresentation in the application for coverage that could render the policy null and void?

If there are no apparent impediments to coverage, the accident investigation begins. If a coverage problem does arise, then the adjuster must put everyone on notice that the investigation is being conducted under the protection of a reservation of rights which means that the company, by continuing the investigation, does not waive any of its rights to challenge coverage at a later date. In cases of sufficient importance, the company may even go to the extent of filing a special lawsuit, asking the court to make a finding, in advance that there is no coverage and the company has no further obligations in the matter at hand. This type of legal action is called a suit for declaratory judgment. In most states, courts have refused to render decisions regarding coverage until the underlying case has been decided since there is reluctance to deprive the insured of his right to defense as promised in the policy.

As soon as the coverage determination has been made, the investigation progresses to the factual circumstances of the accident. The insured is questioned at length, witnesses are interviewed, the accident scene is carefully surveyed, measured and photographed and efforts will be made to collect physical and documentary evidence. In very serious cases, the company will employ professional photographers, engineers and accident reconstruction specialists. This is especially true in cases that arise from public transportation and aircraft accidents. If the adjuster is competent and experienced, no stone will be left unturned to locate any fragment of evidence to reduce or eliminate the financial obligation to the injured party or parties.

Remember, the insurance company's duty is to defend and protect its insured for claims in which this entity may be legally liable. The fundamental purpose of the investigation, therefore, is to determine whether or not there is any possibility of a successful defense or to find additional parties whose participation in the event, might force them to share in the financial obligation to the injured party. For example, you are a passenger in the insured vehicle, making claim against the driver for negligence that caused your injury.

If the accident involves another car, the adjuster will work diligently to find some negligence, no matter how slight, on the part of the other driver in order to bring him or her into the case as a co-defendant. This process arises from a legal doctrine known as contribution among joint tort feasors. It simply means that if more than one party caused your injury, all parties are liable. This brings into the case another company, another adjuster, another attorney, a completely new set of players with each set trying harder than the others are to establish the innocence of their insured.

The final phase of the investigation is directed toward you, your injuries and the damages you have sustained. Your name, address, age, sex and race are submitted to a central index bureau along with as much information about the accident as is available. If you have been injured and made a claim from a previous accident, the information will appear in this archive. It will include the date of the accident, a brief description of your injuries and the name of the company that responded to your claim. Companies frequently share files from previous accidents, so the entire history of the prior claim and its disposition may be available for scrutiny by the current adjuster.

The operative word in this phase of claims handling is control. Repeatedly, the supervisor will ask the adjuster, "Do you have this claimant under control? Does the claimant have your confidence? Are you able to discourage him or her from hiring an attorney? Does he or she cooperate in giving you all the information that we request? "

If the adjuster can respond to these questions in the affirmative, then it is assumed that he has you, the claimant, under his control. By this time, the adjuster will have begun to collect information in the form of documents and reports concerning your injuries, pre-existing conditions, social status, employment and wage data, your current financial condition and whether or not your medical expenses have been paid from another source. In fact, he or she will attempt to develop every scrap of information that might have a bearing on the amount a jury might award if your claim progresses into litigation and goes to actual trial.

If you are alleging an inability to work or participate in sports or recreational activities, and on one particular day, you feel pretty good and decide to play a few holes of golf, don't be too surprised at some later date if you see yourself in the starring role of a short film narrated by your favorite private investigator. Surveillance is still a tactic used by the insurance industry.

As a personal injury victim in an auto accident it is possible that both you and the wrong doer could be insured by the same company or through the same producing agent. This creates an almost certain conflict of interest on the part of the agent, the company and the adjuster. Since this circumstance involves inevitable sharing of information, these cases require special handling and to the extent that it is possible, investigations should be conducted by disinterested parties.

Your own Investigation

Preserving the Evidence

At the earliest possible time following the accident, you, your family or your friends should begin to gather information and documentation to support your claim. In auto accidents, a good starting point is the "police report." It will be on file at the headquarters of the officer or officers who made the on scene investigation, and in most instances, you or your personal representative can make a copy of it. It will contain the date and time of the accident, the precise location where it occurred, the names and addresses of the parties involved, any known witnesses, weather conditions, a brief description of the accident itself and other pertinent facts including traffic violations and citations issued. Photographs of the accident scene from all angles should be taken as well as photographs of the your car and the other vehicle or vehicles involved. The vehicle pictures should depict as nearly as possible the points of impact and the extent of damage showing the severity of the collision. If there are bloodstains on the interior, photograph them. The victim should also have pictures taken that show the nature and extent of injuries, especially to exposed areas of the body where scarring will likely result. The rules of evidence concerning the admission of photographs can be extremely restrictive, so it is advisable to use the services of a commercial photographer who will understand the rules concerning chain of possession, originality and absence of alteration.

You need to find out as much as you can about the responsible party. In addition to their identity it is important to know where they had been and where they were going at the time of the accident. If he or she was traveling in the course of their employment, it is essential to know the name of the employer since the negligence of the employee can lead to responsibility of the employer. This is based upon the common law doctrine that the master is responsible for the acts of his servant. A classic case that demonstrates this doctrine involved a major home delivery pizza company that advertised delivery within a certain number of minutes or there would be no charge for the order. A delivery driver was involved in a serious accident while rushing to meet this deadline and his employer was found liable because the court reasoned that their delivery policy induced dangerous driving on the part of their employees.

You obviously need the wrong doer's address, occupation and as much as you are able to determine about his or her economic status. Does he or she own unencumbered real estate, a business or other substantial wealth?

The emergency medical team who responded to the accident scene might provide information concerning your condition before you were transported to the hospital. Therefore,you should obtain the names and addresses of the ambulance crew. Carefully preserve medical bills, hospital charts, nurses' notes and any other documents related to your treatment.

If the responsible party disputes the facts of the accident it is in your best interest to hire an accident reconstruction expert. This specialist can determine speed at the time of impact, precise point of impact, direction of travel for all involved vehicles, nature and condition of roadway surfaces and other factors that may have contributed to the accident. When these facts are dispute, the professional's testimony can be crucial.

For injuries that result from defective or unreasonably dangerous products, it is important to retain the product in question and have it examined by an appropriate professional who can testify on your behalf. It is also necessary to document the source from which the article was acquired, the date of its purchase, the name and address of the manufacturer, and if it was a component of another item, then the entire device should be preserved. Each piece of evidence should be labeled as to the date it was collected with the label signed by the person in whose possession it will remain. This procedure is to maintain the "chain of custody" record and insure that no tampering takes place before the item is placed in evidence.

In medical malpractice cases you will need to obtain a copy of every chart and note in reference to your treatment including nurses' notes, radiology and laboratory reports, list of medications, discharge summaries and any other documents that set forth the names and addresses of each and every one who participated in your treatment. You must assume that any bit of information, no matter how trivial it may seem, could lend some support to your allegation of medical negligence.

Other professional liability claims such as those involving negligent conduct of attorneys, engineers and accountants, also require as much documentation as you can provide.

Adjusters and Investigators

The claims business in the early fifties was one of the most sexist industries in existence. The only women involved in the investigation and adjustment of claims were secretaries, telephone operators and typists, Like many other occupations that were once the sole province of men, the door to the claims profession widened, and now, there are many women who occupy first line positions in every facet of the business. There is no reason to believe that they are less competent and qualified than their male counterparts, however there remains more than a trace of male dominance in this segment of the insurance industry and it is probable that women are not as well compensated or move as quickly along the career path.

Accompanying the many changes that have taken place in the way companies conduct the investigation and settlement of claims, there has been a noticeable change in the characteristics of adjusters. A question has always existed as to whether or not the position merits the designation professional. Unlike law, medicine and other recognized professions, there is no formal post graduate course of study leading to a degree in claims adjusting, however most companies do require that their adjusters have a college education or its equivalent. In fact, many adjusters have law degrees and use the job as a supplemental training ground, a stepping-stone into the practice of law. The industry, itself, has some programs that are comprehensive, issuing certificates that include the word professional, but for the purpose of compensation, the attitude of the companies does not reflect a sympathetic view. The work of adjusters involves long and arduous hours, absolute integrity and enormous responsibility, yet the remuneration is not commensurate.

Often perceived as excessively biased and suspicious, adjusters are just regular hard working men and women, subject to all the faults and noble attributes that characterize human kind. Early in their careers, they are taught that at least thirty percent of you are exaggerating your injuries or perpetrating outright fraud. This cannot help but introduce elements of cynicism and suspicion into the thought process concerning the trainee's approach to individual claims, and success in the job is not measured by altruistic attitudes. Performance is measured by the expediency and economy in which the employee discharges the task, and the task is to make your cases evaporate from the balance sheet at the lowest possible cost within the confines of the coverage afforded.

During the first two thirds of the last century, the term adjuster was used to describe a person, who handled claims of all types, including property losses such as fire, theft, windstorm, etc. in addition to liability claims for personal injury and property damage. More recently, there has been a trend toward specialization; so that adjusters who handle property losses are less likely to be trained to investigate and handle personal injury claims. Personal injury or liability adjusters are now referred to as claims representatives.

Almost all of the nationally recognized carriers have their own claims staffs, regular salaried employees. Their pay is based upon experience, individual qualifications, performance, length of service with the company and degree of responsibility. Most of the time, these people have the authority to negotiate and settle claims up to a certain dollar limit, and if the claim exceeds that amount, they must obtain more specific authority from a supervisor. If, at the outset, the claim is seen as one involving very serious injuries, it will be assigned to an experienced adjuster. If the initial adjuster discovers, in the course of the investigation, that the dollar amount will ultimately exceed his authority then the claim may be reassigned to someone at a higher settlement level. Some companies routinely reassign claims after a certain time period.

Over the years, the industry has been extremely fortunate in its employment of people who possess the highest degree of integrity; and scandals have been rare. That does not mean that a few adjusters have not gone astray and availed themselves of illicit opportunity involving collusion with rogue attorneys and auto repair concerns. In a large metropolitan area, this practice became so flagrant for a well known company that it became necessary to prohibit its representatives from visiting lawyers' offices. Instead, for negotiating purposes, the attorneys were compelled to come into the claims office to permit monitoring of the negotiations.

Small companies, due to their limited size or lack of volume in a given area, do not maintain widespread claims offices staffed by their own personnel. Instead they employ the services of independent adjusters. These organizations, consisting of as few as one or two people to thousands of employees, exist as private businesses on a worldwide scale. Some operate on a contract basis, handling all of a company's claims for a specific percentage of its premium volume. Most, however, provide their services for an hourly rate plus expenses. These adjusters report to a carrier's central claim office and usually have very little or no authority to commit their principal to a course of action. They simply conduct investigations, report what they have discovered to the company claims department and receive settlement authority or guidance as to further activity.

Former company adjusters have established many of these services and industry groups or associations created others. Wherever you live, you can bet there is an independent adjuster within arms reach.

Since independent adjusters must compete for assignments they are careful to maintain strong relationships with the companies they represent. Because of their need to please the insurance company client, it is probable that their efforts to minimize your settlement will be greater than that of company employees. No matter how sincere these representatives appears to be, you should keep in mind that whatever they might say is designed to promote the ultimate goal, disposition of your claim in a manner most favorable to the company. As has already been suggested, refrain from discussing details of the accident with any of these people, and do not permit a recording of your conversation.. Do not agree to a written signed statement.

Do not sign authorizations to permit the release of medical, employment or wage information to the company. Actually, it is best to sign nothing. In rejecting, these efforts try not to appear antagonistic. Just politely tell the adjuster that you prefer not to disclose the information at this time. The claims process is analogous to a poker game, and you would not want to show your cards before placing the last bet.. Never forget that a personal injury claim is an adversary procedure in which the insurer is trying to achieve a settlement for less than your expectations.

The Investigator

The man sitting in the unfamiliar car parked across the street from your house does not look like anyone from the neighborhood. Maybe he's visiting or just waiting for one of your neighbors? More likely, he's an investigator employed by the insurance company on a surveillance mission. He wants to make you a star in a video production as you walk out the front door carrying your golf clubs or when you push your lawnmower out of the garage to mow your lawn, when you bend over to scrub the tires and wheels on your car, when you twist and turn or lift a heavy object. He wants to catch you doing what you have said you are not able to do because of your injuries. This obscure character in the drama is either a directly employed member of the company claims department or a licensed private investigator. He is probably a former police officer or has had extensive training in the development of information through interrogation or covert observation.

In addition to surveillance, the investigator may interview neighbors and others, often using some form of subterfuge in making such inquiries. Investigations of this type are reserved for cases in which the company suspects malingering or the disability is not consistent with the nature and extent of the claimant's injury.

Some companies also use their own investigators to conduct internal investigations when there is suspicion of fraudulent activity on the part of other company employees or for routine pre-employment background checks.

Structure and Function of the Claims Department

Not all companies are organized in the same way, but they all have a separate department whose principal responsibility is to investigate, settle, deny or defend claims that arise under policies written by the company. The claims department is, in some respects, the eyes and ears of the underwriting department, reporting on the desirability or lack of desirability to retain customers that they encounter in the course of claims handling. Some policies are cancelled based upon information provided by the adjuster. Try getting a couple of moving traffic violations coupled with your accident, and then check your mail for the notice of cancellation.

In very large companies, the home office claims department provides support and supervises branch or regional offices with little or no direct public contact. The executive in charge of this department is usually a senior vice president who reports directly to the chief executive officer and sometimes to a board of directors or a committee within the board. In his or her leadership capacity, this person has the responsibility for developing a departmental budget, appropriate and sufficient staffing, education of personnel, salary administration, public relations, the development of statistical data and, in cooperation with the chief executive officer and the board of directors, the formulation and maintenance of company policy.

You might think that all companies have the same general philosophy regarding the handling of claims, but this is not so. One company may take a very conservative approach, with an all out denial and defense of cases they consider borderline, regardless of cost. The next company may seek to compromise or settle all cases in which the cost of defense will likely exceed the settlement figure. Some companies extend almost unlimited authority to their branch offices for these decisions, while others are more restrictive.

One of the most important functions of the claims department is the establishment of case reserves. Every insurance company must establish reserves for all of its claims, both reported and those that have taken place but not yet reported. The amount of an individual case reserve is set based upon facts developed by the assigned adjuster. There is some flexibility to this procedure and the amount is subject to revision as the investigation progresses. Some companies employ the sophisticated "magic wand" of their actuaries and set up bulk reserves based upon earlier loss experience, premium growth and current trends. Most of the time, this type of reserving is employed in connection with claims that have been incurred but not reported.

A system of average reserving is also used for newly reported claims where there is insufficient information to allocate a specific amount.

The establishment of accurate reserves is a vital function of the claims department and one, which demands careful consideration. One well-known company almost went into bankruptcy due to insufficient reserves, but the industry wide impact of permitting this to occur would have been so adverse that they were "bailed out" with the help of other companies. This company altered its practices and is now an important and profitable component of the industry.

Reserves and Their importance

A reserve is an amount of money set aside for the payment of a future obligation. In this case, we are talking about claims. This amount is treated as a liability on the company's balance sheet as a sum that the company believes will be sufficient to satisfy the claim and the expense of its handling. It is through a combination of paid claims and unpaid loss reserves that a company establishes its loss ratio, the cost of claims to earned premium volume.

Once again policy varies from one company to another with respect to the reserve process. Some companies are excessively optimistic reserving their claims at a very low level while others prefer to err on the high side.

We present this information about reserves because of the role they play in the evaluation and settlement of your claim. Insurance companies cannot tolerate surprises. If a claims department has posted a reserve that fails to satisfy your ultimate settlement or verdict by a wide margin, that is considered a "shock" result that has wide implications. For this reason the adjuster will make a concerted effort to dispose of the claim within the initial reserve. Outcomes of this nature affect other players in the game as will be seen in later chapters of this book dealing with *reinsurance.*

Returning to the way companies conduct their operations, there is often a regional office between the home office and the branch; however it is at the branch or field office that most of the action takes place. Depending upon the geographical area, adjusters may operate from their homes or sub offices located in satellite communities.

In most companies, the branch office will be a full underwriting and production office under the direction of a branch manager. This manager is often almost completely autonomous, accountable to the home office only for profitability and maintaining broad company policy. This pattern of organization is typical of companies that rely upon the independent agency system to market their products. Direct writers, those who sell insurance by mail or telephone, using employee agents are less likely to subordinate central office authority to the same extent.

The branch will simply be a microcosm of the home office. There will be managers for underwriting, marketing, engineering, accounting, human resources, information technology and claims. Each of these will report to the overall branch manager. Some companies separate their claims department, giving it independence from other branch operations, and in those cases the claims manager reports directly to the home office. To some extent this eliminates the influence of marketing over claims decisions.

Among his other responsibilities, the claims manager selects and works in cooperation with outside counsel and adjusters to resolves cases in which suits have been filed. Careful attention must be paid to the timely response to motions and pleadings in these cases and there is always a very fine line between the interests of the company and its insured. In the final analysis, it is incumbent upon the claims manager to protect both. When a major trial takes place, the manager must either attend the trial or remain in close contact with the defense attorney by telephone in the event of attractive settlement opportunities that may present themselves at the last minute.

In recent years, many companies have begun to employ staff attorneys or, so called, house counsel. In addition to other duties, they handle all manner of litigation on behalf of the company and its policyholders, but outside firms are used in major cases or when there is a potential conflict of interest.

Finally, the claims manager is accountable for both quality and production on the part of his or her staff. The ideal is one closed file for each new one assigned with no regulatory complaints. A growing backlog of pending cases assigned to a particular adjuster suggests that some remedial intervention may be in order.

Automobile Property Damage

If your claim arises from a traffic accident for which another driver was to blame and your automobile was damaged, you are entitled to compensation covering the cost to repair or replace it, and, in some cases, its loss of market value as a crash damaged vehicle.If the cost of repairs exceeds or closely approximates the value of the car at the time of the accident, then the vehicle will be deemed a total loss, and its value will be measured by the cost to replace it with a comparable car's retail selling price. Anyone who has bought a used car or negotiated with an automobile salesperson knows the wide latitude in used car values. Most insurance companies use the classified section of local newspapers as a reference to establish values in addition to books published by the auto dealers' trade associations. Mileage and pre accident condition play a role in valuation of your car, and negotiation with the adjuster on this issue is very much like negotiating with a used car salesperson. If your claim also involves personal injuries, however, your automobile claim will be met with less resistance, especially if a difference of opinion might be a detriment to settlement.

The largest limit of liability required for property damage by state regulation is $25,000, and as you can see from the chart in appendix III, this is true of only a handful of states. Most require a meager $10,000 limit or less. Almost any luxury car has a value greater than this, so it may be necessary to present your collision claim on such a vehicle to your own insurance company to have coverage for its true value. Your company, under its right of subrogation, will be entitled to reimbursement to the extent of the responsible party's property damage limit, less the amount of your collision deductible.

There is a controversial and often-overlooked element of damages in automobile property damage claims leaving hundred of thousands, if not millions, of dollars unpaid by insurance companies.

In today's environment, it is virtually impossible to hide the fact that a used car has been involved in a collision even though the repair and restoration has been completed with precision and expertise. Most prospective buyers consult a source called CARFAX where any detrimental information concerning a car such as flood damage, major mechanical problems or collision repairs is easily retrievable.

Does this imply that the value of your new Mercedes is diminished even though the restoration has been properly done? You bet it does. Most people will be hesitant about buying a car with a history of collision involvement regardless of the repair quality. The percentage of value diminution depends on the make, model and age of the vehicle in question, but it is a virtual certainty that a car with an accident history will have a trade-in or resale value that is less than a pristine similar model.

There are mixed decisions by the courts regarding coverage for loss of value in the standard auto policy covering the car for collision damage. Courts in the majority of states have ruled that the language in the standard ISA auto policy is unambiguous and does not contemplate payment for post repair devaluation. However, this is not true in claims against a responsible parties or their insurance company. In most states, courts have ruled that diminution in value is a legitimate element of damage. A few states still maintain the position that the difference in market value before and after the accident is resolved by the cost to repair the damage.

In any event, you or your attorney should consider this additional loss as you pursue your personal injury and property damage claim. *If the cost to repair your classic Corvette will exhaust the responsible party's property damage limit of liability, then you should present the collision claim to your own carrier and , under the made whole doctrine, collect your deductible and claim for diminished value from the responsible party's insurer. Under the so called made whole doctrine, you are entitled to collect all of your uninsured losses before your insurer asserts its right of subrogation for the amount of your collision claim. This will leave the responsible party's property damage limit to respond to your diminished value claim and your insurer is left with the remainder, if anything, for its subrogation claim.*

The selection of a well-qualified repair facility is obviously an important consideration. There is both quality and slip shod workmanship in the market place. Some major insurance companies have negotiated contracts with preferred body shops who will work with company appraisers to effect repairs at the lowest possible cost, and this may include the use of after market parts or used parts instead of equipment provided by the manufacturer. This may be appropriate in some older vehicles, but you should understand that you are not compelled to use one of the facilities recommended by the insurer. The choice is yours. You do not have to accept substandard repairs.

In the destruction that takes place in an automobile accident, the vehicle's contents such as clothing and other personal property is frequently lost, damaged or destroyed. These items such as jewelry, watches, cameras and computers can represent substantial losses and you should not overlook them in the presentation of your claim.

In addition to all of the foregoing, you are entitled to reimbursement for a rental car for as long as it takes to repair or replace your own vehicle. Insurance companies have agreements with most of the major car rental companies to provide certain vehicles for a discounted daily rate. If your car is a full sized luxury model, then you are entitled to a comparable rental unit. You are not required to accept a lesser vehicle to accommodate the insurer's discount arrangement. The rental company will sometimes require the purchase of insurance to cover their vehicle for a substantial daily premium, and this too, can be included in your damage claim against the responsible party.

Temporary Financial Resources

There are a number of available resources to ease your financial burden while you are waiting for final settlement, and you should make a diligent effort to determine their availability.

Workers Compensation Insurance

If you were working at the time of the accident, your employers workers compensation insurance will pay all of your medical expenses and a percentage of your lost wages. When your case is settled by the responsible party's insurance carrier, the Workers Compensation carrier will be entitled to reimbursement from the proceeds of your settlement, but more often than not the WC carrier will accept less than their total expenditures if their claim represents an impediment to your settlement. For example, assume that the other party's liability policy has a limit of $500,000 and the workers compensation company has paid out more than that amount on your behalf. You refuse to settle unless you are assured that you will receive some part of the available $500,000. In that situation, it is entirely possible that the WC carrier will accept less than its overall payout, leaving the balance for you and your attorney.

Your personal auto policy

You are entitled to recover the cost to repair or replace your car or any other property damaged in the accident as well as the cost to rent a comparable replacement vehicle while your car is being repaired or replaced. If your policy includes collision insurance, you can present a claim under that policy, and at the time of settlement your company will be repaid from the proceeds of your settlement. Your auto company derives its right to be reimbursed under the clause in your policy entitled "Subrogation" which is a legal doctrine providing for assignment to the insurance company that part of your claim which has been paid under the coverage provided by your own policy.

Your policy may also contain medical payments coverage, entitling you to reimbursement for medical expenses up to the stated limit; usually $2,000. to $5000. In states that have enacted so called "no fault" laws the policy will also include coverage for a percentage of wage loss as well as a percentage of reasonable and necessary medical expenses. This coverage called personal injury protection, also provides reimbursement for replacement services, meaning those things which the insured would normally provide for his household were it not for his injury such as meal preparation, household maintenance, laundry, etc.

Health Insurance

You should notify your health carrier as soon as possible after the accident. Hospital and other bills covering your treatment will start coming in very soon, and it is in your best interest to have them paid as soon as possible. Some accident and health policies also provide for a lump sum payment for each day a patient is hospitalized; however it is advisable to have the language in these contracts carefully scrutinized, for "all that glitters is not gold." As in the case of your auto policy, the provider of your health insurance will seek reimbursement from the responsible party's insurance carrier.

Social Security Disability

If your injury will cause you to be totally disabled (unable to perform any gainful employment) for at least one year following the accident, you are entitled to SSI disability compensation. The amount of your monthly payment from this source will depend on your work history and the amount of your earnings. File your claim with Social Security as soon as possible since *the wheels of government turn slowly*, and it may take several months to reach a decision as to acceptance or rejection of your claim.

Medicare and Medicaid

If you have no health insurance and your accident does not qualify you for workers' compensation benefits, it is possible that the cost of your treatment will be covered under Medicare or Medicaid. You can make an inquiry for this benefit through the local Social Security office where you reside.

Statutes of Limitation

All 50 states and the federal government have statutes that set forth limits on the period that a party who has suffered injury or property damage has in which to file a lawsuit against the wrongdoer. Except in cases where the statute is suspended, if suit is not filed within the specified time, then the injured party has no further recourse. If you have an attorney and he fails to file before the statute runs, then it is likely that you will have a claim against the attorney for professional negligence.

If the defendant (wrongdoer) is absent from the court's jurisdiction, the statute may be suspended and will not start to run until his return.

In some states, a suit against the estate of a deceased defendant may require the appointment of an executor or administrator within a certain period of time that may be considerably shorter than the statute of limitations. This deserves careful attention by your attorney. A lapse might be fatal to your case.

We have purposely omitted a chart showing the statute of limitations for every state territory and the District of Columbia since these laws change with some degree of regularity and circumstances of individual claims may have a bearing on the time period allotted for filing suit;

To be on the safe side, you should consult with an attorney as soon after an accident as possible to determine if any special limitations apply to your claim.

Workers' Compensation

All 50 states, the District of Columbia and the Federal government require employers to provide workers compensation insurance to cover injuries to their employees arising out of their employment. There is an entire body of law surrounding claims arising from employment related injuries, and each state is unique in the benefits provided and procedure for claims decisions. The workers compensation insurance policy simply provides the resources from which the employer pays the benefits to which the injured employee is entitled. The policy must conform to the law in the jurisdiction where the claim is presented.

Unlike liability and property insurance contracts, there are few conditions and exclusions, and the only monetary limitations are those that are set forth in the law itself.

Workers compensation laws provide for partial payment of an employee's wages during a period of temporary or permanent disability that is the result of a work related injury. In the event an employee dies because of his injury, compensation is paid to his dependent spouse or children. In addition, the injured employee is entitled to full and complete medical care necessitated by his injury. This is a lifetime benefit and includes nursing care, home health services, special equipment, prosthetic devices and any modifications to the home that are required to accommodate that employee's handicap.

Prior to the enactment of workers compensation legislation in the early twentieth century, an employee's only recourse for an injury suffered at work were the civil justice system's tort laws. It was necessary to sue the employer and prove his negligence caused your injury before there could be any recovery. This was often difficult, if not impossible, to prove and left the employee without income or the ability to pay medical expenses or rehabilitation costs. Under workers compensation laws, the employee gives up his right to sue his employer in exchange for the benefits provided above.

While the amount is not universally true, most state workers compensation laws provide disability payments up to two thirds of the employee's average weekly wage during the continuation of total disability and a lesser amount for partial disability after the employee reaches maximum medical improvement.

In the event of an employee's death resulting from a work related accident, the widow and dependent children are entitled to benefits. These benefits are usually terminated if and when the widow remarries and the dependent children reach majority.

Some states permit an injured worker to select his own physician while others mandate treatment by a designated doctor or one from a list provided by the employer. In cases where the employer contests disability ratings, it is likely that the employee will need to consult with his own doctor in order to challenge the rating provided by the company physician.

When you suffer a work related injury, must report the accident to his workers compensation carrier and the state board or commission that provides administration for the state's workers compensation system. If the injury prevents you from working, you are entitled to an award for temporary total disability. The laws usually provide for a short waiting period before compensation If the disability continues after the waiting period for another specified period, then compensation for the waiting period is paid retroactively. In most jurisdictions in the United States, there is also a provision for continued payment of compensation for permanent partial and permanent total disability if such disability continues to exist after you have reached maximum medical improvement.

In contested cases, the hearing commissioner or administrative law judge will render decisions on both fact and law. The decisions may be subject to appeals to an appropriate state court; however, there is usually a presumption that the findings at the administrative level were correct, and the burden of proof to the contrary rests with the employer and the insurance company.

Many times an employee's injuries are caused by the negligent act of a party other than the employer or a fellow employee. In these circumstances, the employee has a cause of action in tort against the responsible party as well as a statutory claim under workers compensation. As we explained earlier, the workers compensation insurance carrier is entitled to reimbursement of any payments to or on behalf of the injured employee from any settlement or judgment against the third party. In some cases it may be in the interest of the workers compensation insurer to waive its right to recovery/ Such an agreement might be reached with an injured employee as part of a final compromise to terminate future benefits. Some part of the tort settlement would include payment for general damages such as pain and suffering that are not included under workers' compensation.

Statutes and case law in connection with workers compensation are voluminous, and it is impossible to touch on every aspect of the subject in a work such as this.

Because of the diverse and complex nature of the law, anyone who has suffered a work related injury that could result in complete or partial disability whether temporary or permanent should absolutely seek the services of an attorney who specializes in workers compensation claims in the involved jurisdiction.

States regulate attorney's fees in these cases; and the fee is paid from the award of compensation. This does not mean that some negotiation is out of the question. If, upon review, the attorney finds that there are no issues that must be resolved at a hearing and the claim is not be contested by the employer or the insurance carrier, then it would not be appropriate for him to charge the full percentage allowed by the state. For example, an employee dies because of a clearly compensable accident, leaves a fully dependent widow and several dependent children. The statute provides specific benefits for the widow and dependent children, and if the employer insurance carrier are not contesting any part of the claim, an ethical attorney would inform his client that his services will not be needed, charge a reasonable fee for his review and advise the client to accept the benefits provided under the statute.

For those who wish to pursue the law of workers compensation in depth, the accepted authority is Larson's Workers' Compensation Law that can be found in your local circuit court law library.

Hiring an Attorney

This is, perhaps, the most important step in the claims process. If your injury is severe, the catastrophe is your nightmare, but it could be the bonanza that some attorney or firm of attorneys has dreamed about since their admission to the bar.

Care in the selection and hiring of an attorney cannot be overstated. We offer a number of suggestions regarding this step in the process, and are confident that if the guidelines set forth are followed, the successful search for and employment of the right attorney for a particular case will be much more likely. Not every practicing lawyer has the energy, knowledge and professional expertise to come up against the best the insurance company has to offer. While it is true that most cases are settled out of court, the fact remains that every claim is a potential lawsuit and should be looked upon in that light. If your attorney's standing in the system is well known by both the insurance industry and the defense bar, it will have an impact on the value of your case.

Attorneys provide their services in personal injury cases under contingent fee contracts. This arrangement means that you will pay nothing unless your case results in a recovery of money damages from the responsible party or their insurance company. The attorney will then receive an agreed upon percentage of your settlement or award. The percentage can be in a range anywhere from 25% to 50%, so you are, in effect, establishing a partnership with your attorney in a mutually beneficial enterprise. The typical contingent fee contract calls for 25% of the amount recovered in settlement before suit is filed and 33 1/3 % after filing; even if the case is settled without trial. Many personal injury attorneys automatically establish the higher fee arrangement by filing suit immediately after employment.

There was a time when most state or county bar associations published minimum fee schedules, imposing minimums that lawyers were permitted to charge their clients for certain services. For the most part these limitations have been abandoned since there have been decisions that they violate anti trust laws.

So let us pose a simple question. If you were an attorney seeking to represent a client with an iron clad seven figure case: for example a person with a paralyzing spinal cord injury, blindness, brain damage, horrible scarring or death, would you refuse to represent the client for less than the usual and customary twenty-five to fifty percent? Assuming the responsible party has the resources to pay such an award, only a fool would fail to see that ten to fifteen percent of a huge sum is much better than zero percent of nothing. The lawyer will argue that he is betting his time and expenses against an uncertain outcome with the possibility of a low or even zero verdict. Do you remember what was said earlier about jury verdicts? Never forget that the result of a jury trial is completely unpredictable.

In your fee negotiations, you might want to consider telling the attorney that you will agree to pay his fee based upon a percentage of any verdict or settlement greater than your actual "out of pocket" expense or over and above the insurance carrier's best offer. Assuming your medical expenses and lost income are $40,000; you immediately increase your potential net recovery by $10,000. In any event, the door is open for negotiation before you sign the representation agreement, and I seriously doubt that, in the type of cases I have described, the client will leave the lawyer's office without a more favorable fee arrangement than the attorney's first offer. None of this applies unless the wrong doer's assets or insurance limits are sufficient to pay a mammoth verdict. A verdict against an indigent defendant is essentially worthless.

Among other criteria, you want to select someone with a proven track record. In how many cases has he actually gone to trial? How many of these trials resulted in verdicts for the plaintiffs (victims) that were greater than the defendant's best offer?

Does the attorney or the law firm maintain a war chest with adequate resources to pay expert witnesses and other expenses? You may need an economist to project your loss of income over the rest of your expected working life, the cost of your care adjusted for inflationary factors, a medical specialist to testify concerning the nature and extent of your disability, pain and suffering and potentially shortened life expectancy. Experts come at a high price.

Does the firm have available witnesses who are professionally qualified and have unblemished records in their fields of endeavor? These witnesses should be practicing members of their professions, not deriving their income principally from testifying in personal injury cases.

It is not in your best interest to hire a lawyer who is desperate for cash. Many cases have been settled earlier and for less money than they should have been simply because the lawyer needed money for taxes or other obligations. In this connection, insurance companies frequently obtain credit reports on plaintiffs' attorneys and their clients to assess their financial status.

Ask for references and a list of cases in which major corporations or insurance companies have suffered defeat in their opposition to the attorney. Some of this information may be available to the public through the courts, the local bar association or the press. You might even want to consider going to a nationally known firm such as the Melvin Belli firm domiciled in San Francisco for many years and considered the nemesis of the insurance industry. Another great source for exploration is the World Wide Web. Simply insert the phrase *multi-million dollar jury verdicts* in your browser, and you will find dozens of successful firms and attorneys.

Many personal injury attorneys have further limited their practices to particular areas of the law such as medical malpractice, products liability, common carrier cases involving airline accidents and other public transportation claims. Nevertheless, hundreds of attorneys still handle cases of all types.

You are not likely to find the most qualified attorney for your case in a small town or rural setting. The demographics will simply not generate enough important litigation to support a lawyer with five star credentials. You should probably concentrate your search in a city or urban area that has at least a half million population. If the case is to be tried in a "home town" setting, your selected counsel can and probably will associate with a local firm because familiarity with judges, jury panels and local court rules are important considerations in a lawsuit.

Like it or not, age, ethnicity and physical appearance all contribute to a lawyer's success or failure in the courtroom. Your attorney must be able to make the jury feel your pain and evoke their sympathy. His perception by the jury carries a lot of weight.. Every personal injury or wrongful death case has unique characteristics. The successful lawyer will know how and when to use these imponderables to your advantage, conveying a sense of outrage or quiet humility as necessary. His performance should be like that of an accomplished actor.

There was a time when advertising and the solicitation of clients was an ethical breach known as barratry, the offense of stirring up quarrels and promoting litigation. One need only open the yellow pages or turn on a television to see that this restriction has fallen by the wayside. There is little doubt that the weakening of this ethical standard has promoted the public's perception of personal injury lawyers as greedy ambulance chasing vultures. Make no mistake about it, however, they occupy an imperative *r*ole in our civil justice system and in their absence, there would be no compensation for any innocent personal injury or property damage victim. With or without his retention in a case, the mere availability of a lawyer, if needed, is an important deterrent to outrageous conduct by the insurer The existence of a highly successful attorney in the negotiating process introduces a *fear factor* that will play a major role in the settlement result.

Most of the foregoing applies only to the catastrophically injured victim and his family. Minor injuries, while not trivial, do not fall into the category that requires the services of heavyweight law firms.

The victim can successfully negotiate many of these cases without hiring an attorney whose services may consist of nothing more than a letter or two and a telephone call to the claims adjuster.

Claims of this nature are the bread and butter of the average law firm, but there is serious question as to how much a lawyer improves the result in small to moderate cases. If the difference between the insurance company's best offer and the injured party's demand is only a few thousand dollars, then it is likely that the fee for a lawyer's services and the potential delay in settlement will offset the reduction in the settlement amount. For example, the adjuster has made you an offer of $15,000. You will accept no less than $20,000. If you hire a lawyer, you will sign a contingent fee agreement for no less than 25% of the award, so if he is able to recover an additional $5000., it will simply pay the lawyer's fee, and you could still be obligated for some expenses, court filing fees, deposition transcripts, service of subpoenas, etc.

It is reasonable to expect that any individual who has completed a course of study in a recognized college of law and has successfully passed a comprehensive examination for admission to the bar is certifiably intelligent, disciplined and, at least, minimally competent to practice the profession. There probably are no stupid lawyers. The educational requirements are too demanding. Unfortunately, there is no test to guarantee or predict flawless and unequivocal character. Lawyers are human, and humans are less than perfect. Therefore, the final caveat that I will offer here is use extreme caution in the employment of legal counsel. Beware of television advertising. Understand the difference between trial lawyers and settlement mills. There are plenty of lawyers, not very many great ones, and they are in stiff competition for clients. Do not expect a goldfish to do the work of a shark. Above all, do not hesitate to engage in fee negotiations.

Settlement

Your medical treatment is completed. You know the full extent of any residual disability. You know the precise amount of your out of pocket expenses and loss of income because of the accident, and you are ready to settle. You, alone, or you and your attorney have reached an agreement with the insurance company on the amount of your claim.

Settlement is possible in almost any way that is agreeable between the parties. First, there is the straightforward, single payment method in which you will be required to sign a full release for any existing or future claims in exchange for a specific sum of money. The company will then issue a check or draft in that amount payable to you or to you and your attorney if you are represented. Before you sign the release, be certain that you are not extinguishing your rights against other persons who may have contributed to your injury. For example, in a medical malpractice action, your claim may be against a number of entities such as one or more physicians, a hospital, a laboratory or others. If you settle your claim independently with just one of the wrong doers, it is likely that you have reduced the amount of your recovery by the extent of the sum paid by the single tort feasor. Contribution among tort feasors who are jointly and severally liable for injuries and damage is a relatively complex legal concept and one that requires the services of a competent attorney.

While it should not be necessary to include this caveat, you need to be certain that the amount of the insurance company's check is consistent with the sum for which you have agreed to settle. Your attorney will have you endorse the check, deduct the amount of his fee plus any expenses for which you are responsible and then issue his own check to you for the balance. Look at both the front and the back of the check before you endorse it, and under no circumstances permit the attorney to present the check for payment, as your attorney, without your endorsement. Yes, although it is unlikely, this implies that there is a very slight risk of fraudulent behavior on the part of your own lawyer. Most lawyers are honest and ethical, but they are also human.

Another option is the structured settlement. In this type of settlement, the defendant's insurer usually purchases an annuity through a life insurance company that will make periodic payments to the injured party over a long period. As suggested by the term *structured*, this type of settlement can be designed in a variety of forms to meet the needs of the claimant. For example, there can be a lump sum paid up front to cover immediate expenses such as medical treatment , special equipment and, of course, attorney fees. The balance of the money is used to purchase an annuity for future periodic payments. If you agree to defer periodic payments for a long term before they commence, then the amount available grows according to the time value of money. The future value of an annuity is calculated using some algebraic formulae, taking into consideration all of the known variables.

Structured settlements are especially beneficial in the case of claimants who might be likely to waste a large lump sum payment or for minors who have no immediate need for the cash.

For beneficiaries who become dissatisfied with the periodic payment arrangement or those who develop an urgent need for cash, an opportunistic service recently presented through television advertising, shows people yelling from windows, "It's my money and I need it now!" No precise details are given, but it is probable that the advertisers are offering lump sums at a discounted rate in exchange for the annuities. Whether or not a person should choose this option depends upon the size of the discount and the degree of urgency in the need for immediate cash. An important consideration is that the offer will be substantially less than the present value of the annuity.

Before agreeing to a structured settlement, you should be certain that the annuity is obtained from a major life insurance company with a strong financial rating.

To be valid, the personal injury claim of a minor requires court approval. This involves the appointment of a guardian ad litem (usually one of the parents) who is charged with the responsibility to oversee a trust fund that is created for the injured child. This is to prevent improper disposition of the settlement fund. Ordinarily the trust terminates when the claimant attains majority. Insurance companies have routinely ignored this requirement in claims involving trivial injuries and payments that are less than $1,000. They have simply had the parents execute a release called a Parents guardian release and indemnity agreement This type of settlement is a calculated risk on the part of an insurance company since some states mandate the appointment of a guardian to safeguard the child's interests. It is possible that a person whose claim was settled in this manner by his parent could still maintain his own cause of action upon reaching majority unless the statute of limitations has run, usually the personal injury time period following the minor's twenty-first birthday.

For example, the parents of a 16 year old settle his personal injury claim for a trivial amount by signing a release as his parents or legal guardians. A few years later, a complication arises. What appeared to be a minor injury has resulted in a serious condition that requires further treatment, leaving some permanent disability. It is possible that the earlier settlement could be set aside and the claimant could proceed with his own claim. The only relief for the wrong doer or his insurer would be an offset from any judgment for the earlier settlement.

When suit is filed against multiple defendants, there are sometimes special agreements with one or more of the defendants known as Mary Carter Agreements and High Low agreements. The Mary Carter agreement arises from the Florida appeals court case of Booth v. Mary Carter Paint Company. It provides for a secret agreement made between a plaintiff and one or more but not all co-defendants in a personal injury lawsuit. In such an agreement, all of the defendants continue as parties to the suit, guaranteeing a minimum payment to the plaintiff for an agreed amount if no award is made against the other non-settling defendants. The plaintiff, in exchange, agrees to offset their liability by or to paythem from a recovery awarded against the other defendants. Some states have ruled that such agreements are illegal, while others will permit them with disclosure to the jury.

High Low agreements provide an agreement between the plaintiff and defendant that the award will be no less than a low figure and no more than an agreed high. These agreements usually take place only when there is a reasonable certainty of a judgment against the defendant. Such an agreement is favorable to an insurance carrier and its insured to prevent an award in excess of the policy limits. High low agreements are legal in all jurisdictions.

The Lawsuit and Civil Jury Trial

You have decided that your claim cannot be settled for what you think it's worth. You have reached a satisfactory agreement with an attorney concerning his fees. You have determined that the wrong doer(s) have sufficient assets to cover a judgment, and you have authorized the filing of suit. Your attorney will prepare a document known as a complaint to be filed in the court that has jurisdiction in your case, usually the state and county where the accident took place. There are a number of exceptions to this, but your attorney will know the proper venue for your case. The complaint will name all defendants against whom you are filing, a brief description of the negligent act or acts that form the basis for which you are seeking money damages and an amount that you are asking the court to award known as an ad damnum.

A copy of each complaint and a summons ia served on each defendant who will be given an opportunity to file an answer, usually within thirty days of service. Most of the time the answer will simply be a succinct denial that the defendant committed the wrongs alleged or the complaint fails to state a cause of action upon which relief can be granted. Failure on the part of a defendant to file an answer may result in a default judgment upon the filing of such a motion by you, the plaintiff; however it will still be incumbent upon you to prove your damages.

The next step following service of the summons and complaint and the defendant(s) answer is the process known as discovery. Each party to the suit is given an opportunity to seek information from the other concerning evidence which either intends to introduce at the trial. The attorneys for both parties prepare questions known as interrogatories that pertain to evidence that will be introduced at trial. Both parties may request the production of documents, the names and addresses of all prospective witnesses and may include a requirement by the plaintiff to submit to physical examinations.

Depositions of parties and witnesses named in the interrogatories usually follow. The deposition is testimony under oath taken before a court reporter (sometimes a video camera) and will be used in the trial during direct and cross-examination. Any variance between the testimony at trial and the deposition can be used to challenge the information provided by the witness.

In the course of and at the completion of the discovery process, which may be subject to a time limit or cut off date, there will be motions filed by both sides regarding legal or procedural issues that must be decided by the court. A pre-trial conference usually follows during which the judge will make every effort to persuade both parties to reach a settlement agreement. If this fails, the court will, in most jurisdictions, order the parties to undertake mediation Just as at trial, the case will be presented before an impartial mediator who will render a non-binding verdict. If either of of the parties rejects the mediator's decision, then the lawsuit will continue to trial.

Before the curtain rises, let's take a look at the cast of characters for this bizarre theatre. At center stage is the person in the black robe seated appropriately behind an elevated bench. He or she is the director of this production. The Hollywood version of this player usually depicts him or her as the personification of pompous stoicism. This is not necessarily true. Some judges actually have a keen sense of humor. In addition to his duty to maintain order and decorum, the judge, referred to as the court, has a primary responsibility for ruling on matters of law and procedure.

Unseen in the background, the judge will have a clerk, usually a recent law school graduate, who will assist with legal research and provide support to the judge in formulating and writing opinions.

The armed, uniformed figure standing near the bench is the bailiff. His job is to provide security in the courtroom, announce the entrance of judges, prevent contact with the public by jurors, and remove or arrest people who disrupt the proceedings.

Seated at a table nearest to the bench, is the court reporter or stenographer whose duty is to record every word that is spoken in the course of the trial and maintain a written record should its transcription become necessary. Sometimes, the shorthand record is supplemented by electronic media recording.

Next there is a table for the court clerk who will mark exhibits that are offered in evidence and perform other administrative tasks such as maintaining and retrieving records, collecting fines, issuing subpoenas, etc.

In front of the railing that separates the public seating area there are two tables side by side. One is for you and your attorney and the other is for the defendant and his or her attorney. The questioning of witnesses is usually done from these tables unless the court grants permission for an attorney to approach the witness. The attorney may stand before the jury during the course of their opening and closing arguments. They may not approach the bench at any time without first seeking permission from the judge, and when this occurs, such a conference requires the presence of all participating counsel. This discussion, taking place outside the earshot of the jury, is known as a sidebar conference.

On one side of the courtroom, usually the same side as the plaintiff's table, there are two rows of seats that are slightly elevated. This is where the jury of six to 12 persons and one alternate will sit. Witnesses, unless they are excluded from hearing the testimony of others, may be seated in the public seating area.

With all the characters in place, the drama begins. A panel of prospective jurors is selected from the public by a lottery system, usually from voter registrations. The selection of the six or twelve jurors and one alternate to hear your case will then begin with the *voir dire* procedure. In this phase, each attorney has an opportunity to question prospective jurors to determine their qualifications to hear the case. Both plaintiff and defendant are entitled to three peremptory (without cause) challenges in which they may strike or disqualify any prospective juror. Your attorney will make these choices based upon how he would like the jury to be constituted for any number of factors such as ethnicity, age, occupation, or sex. All of the other challenges are for cause. For example, the juror might be related to or personally acquainted with one of the parties or attorneys. He or she may have prior knowledge about the case and express an opinion that would render him/her unable to render an impartial verdict.

Throughout all of this questioning and selection process, the attorneys do not wish to appear intimidating or argumentative since this is their first opportunity to present themselves to the jury that will decide your case. The questions will be polite and gentle.

The courtroom is usually arranged so that tables are positioned on each side, and your table, as plaintiff, will be situated next to the jury box. The seating arrangement leaves you and your attorney exposed to constant scrutiny throughout the trial. This makes it extremely important to avoid improper gestures and facial expressions. It is a time for stoicism.

After the jury is sworn and takes their seats, the trial begins with opening statements. Representing you as the plaintiff, your attorney will be first to address the jury. He will explain what the defendant did or failed to do that caused your injury and outline the evidence he will present, which he believes will prove your allegations. None of his remarks will constitute evidence or proven facts for consideration by the jury at this stage of the trial. Next the defendant's attorney makes his opening statement in which he will attempt to refute the allegations made by your attorney.

Now comes the presentation of evidence. Again, as plaintiff, you and your witnesses will take the stand first. There will be direct questioning by your attorney followed by cross-examination from the defendant's attorney. If there are documents or physical evidence like charts, photographs or other objects to be introduced, they will be marked as exhibits by the clerk and presented to the judge for their admission before they are given to the jury for their examination. During the questioning, either on direct examination by your attorney or cross examination by the defendant's attorney, there may be objections to certain questions or to the introduction of a document or item of physical evidence. It will be the responsibility of the trial judge to rule upon these objections. Most of the time, objections are made concerning testimony by witnesses about matters which he/she has no direct knowledge, information that was given to the witness by someone else. Testimony of this kind is known as hearsay, and it is usually not admissible.

There is no limit to the number of witness that may be called by either side. A list of witnesses is submitted before the trial, and if another witness is called who is not on this list, some courts will require that the party calling the surprise witness, show that the he was not discovered until after a pre trial conference. It is usually within the discretionary power of a trial judge to exclude such a witness from testifying.

After the introduction of the evidence and all of the testimony is complete, either or both sides may submit motions, requesting the court to render favorable decisions. This will be followed by closing arguments. Your attorney will speak first, summarizing the evidence, including facts of the accident and the extent of your injuries and damages. He will then ask the jury to render a verdict on your behalf, awarding the money damages that you demanded in your initial pleading. The defendant's lawyer will be next to address the jury. He will challenge the facts of the accident as well as the nature and extent of your injuries. Like your own attorney, he will ask the jury to render a decision that is favorable to his client

Finally, before the jury is sent to deliberate, the judge issues instructions to them covering the law of the case and some standard instructions on how they should proceed. Usually the attorneys for both sides provide the court with suggested instructions based upon their research of statutes and precedent cases. The jury then retires to the jury room where they elect a foreperson and begin to review the evidence that has been presented by both sides. Unlike criminal cases where conviction depends upon proof beyond a reasonable doubt, the civil jury in a personal injury lawsuit can base their decision upon a preponderance of evidence. This means that the jury gives more weight to the evidence presented by one side as opposed to the other, even if the difference is only slight. Some, but not all, states mandate that a jury verdict in a personal injury case be unanimous. If no agreement can be made, then the jury is said to be deadlocked and the judge will declare a mistrial. The case will then have to be retried with a new jury or dismissed.

If a verdict is reached, the foreperson will inform the bailiff who will, in turn, inform the judge. The jury will then return to the jury box where the judgment will be announced. In the absence of appeals by either side, the case is ended. If the award is outrageous or does not conform to limitations provided by statute, the trial judge has the authority to reduce the amount, order a complete new trial or a trial on the issue of damages only.

Collection of Judgments

Now comes some good news and some bad news.. The good news is that if the party who caused your injury has insurance with sufficient limits and there is no appeal, you will be paid promptly by the insurance company with a draft payable to you and your attorney. The attorney will deduct his fee and give you a check for the balance.

The bad news, in cases arising from automobile accidents, is that there are many uninsured and underinsured motorists recklessly cruising the streets and highways of America. If the person responsible for the accident that brought about your injuries is a male driver under 25, operating his own car, the probability that he is uninsured or does not have adequate limits increases exponentially. Every state has a law requiring automobile liability coverage, but the limits required are pitifully inadequate, usually not sufficient to pay the medical expenses of a victim for the first few days in the hospital. The highest required limit for any state, as of this writing, is the state of Maine, which requires $50,000. per person, $100,000 per accident and $25,000 for property damage. The required limits in the remaining states may be seen in appendix III in addition to the address and telephone number for each of the state departments of insurance.

Therefore, if your accident involves a person insured with Maine's limits and you happen to be driving a new Mercedes and are be hospitalized for thirty days, you have a potential insurance recovery in amount of $75,000. This amount will cover only a fraction of your actual expenses and even less if the accident occurs in one of the other states.

Although a great many of the health and accident insurers who market accidental death and disability policies are suspect, there are some who are legitimate and faithfully honor their contracts. Considering the inadequacy of automobile insurance in response to a serious injury, it might be advisable for the family breadwinner or winners to consider this additional protection. Remember the adage, *"You can't get blood out of a turnip."*

You probably will not know the available limits of the wrongdoer's liability insurance coverage at the outset of your claim, but in most states, this information is available by simply making the request in writing or, in the alternative, through the discovery process when litigation begins.

PART II

Insured Property Claims

Homeowners Claims

For most people, the home and its contents are their most valuable assets. It follows that insurance coverage for them is of extreme importance. If there is a mortgage, then the mortgage company will require a homeowner's policy with sufficient coverage on the dwelling to cover at least the unpaid balance.

Coverage of the Homeowners Policy

Make a claim and we'll cancel your policy. Probably not, but if you are unprofitable for a policy period (one year or three years) there is a strong likelihood that your company will not renew your policy. If you are a bartender, cocktail waitress or a celebrity of any kind, expect to pay more for your insurance coverage. If you live in a state where natural disasters occur frequently, wholesale cancellations and non renewals are commonplace.

The word policy is technically a misnomer for this coverage, since it is really a package containing a collection of policies. The homeowners' coverage was first introduced in the 1950s, a creation of one of the country's leading property-casualty insurance companies. Previously there were separate policies covering fire and lightning with riders or endorsements to include windstorm, hail and a few other perils such as vandalism and malicious mischief. Theft coverage was only covered if the consumer purchased a personal property floater. Not everyone could qualify for this coverage as companies were extremely selective and it was expensive, written mostly to cover jewelry, furs, silverware and other valuable artifacts. In order to have protection from legal liability as provided in section II of the homeowners policy it was necessary to purchase a comprehensive personal liability policy. To separately produce this array of policies was both unwieldy and expensive, so along came the homeowners policy that packaged all the coverage under a single cover with one premium.

The basic homeowners policy is a named perils form, covering only those perils listed such as fire and lightning and the windstorm and hail extensions that formed a part of the earlier separate policies. Most consumers purchase the broad form which provides coverage for "all risks of physical damage" except those that are excluded such as flood, earth movement (including earthquake) war, nuclear hazards and several additional causes of damage such as normal wear and tear, acts of civil authorities, weather conditions and intentional loss arising out of any act " committed by or at the direction of an insured."

In most forms and in most states, personal property is not covered for replacement cost unless the election is made by the insured to purchase the personal property replacement cost endorsement. This endorsement has a number of exceptions and limitations which will be discussed further in this section.

In addition to the exclusions there are further limitations to coverage of certain property, and it is strongly suggested that you read the_Section I Conditions and the paragraph that reads *loss settlement* This is where the you will find the language in which the company substitutes its promised payment for replacement cost without deduction for depreciation to actual cash value until the property has been repaired or replaced. Let's assume that your digital camera for which you paid $1,000.00 three years ago has been stolen. The replacement cost for one of like kind and quality has now risen to $1200.00. Since the camera has a value greater than $500.00, its loss will be adjusted on an actual cash value basis until you actually replace the camera and provide proof of your purchase.If your policy has a deductible greater than the ACV or fair market value of the used camera, then you would get nothing until replacement and then only the excess over the deductible.

With respect to buildings under coverage A and B, you must purchase coverage equal to or greater than 80% of the cost to replace your home or any restoration costs will be subject to depreciation. Here is a simplified example. Replacement cost of your home at the time of loss is determined to be $200,000. In order to receive a loss settlement based upon the cost to repair or replace without depreciation, your policy on your dwelling, must be at least $160,000. Assuming that you choose a lesser amount, then the loss will be adjusted in accordance with the loss settlement conditions as follows:

"If at the time of loss, the amount of insurance on the damaged building is less than 80% of the replacement cost of the building immediately before the loss, we will pay the greater of the following amounts, but not more than the limit of liability under this policy that applies to the building."

The actual cash value of that part of the building damaged, or(b) That proportion of the cost to repair or replace after application of the deductible and without deduction for depreciation, that part of the building damaged wich the total amount of insurance in this policy of the damaged building bears to 80% of the replacement cost of the building.

In other words, if you insure for less than 80% of replacement cost, suffer a loss to some part of your home that is subject to normal wear and tear such as a roof, paint or wallpaper, then it is likely that you will not collect the full cost to replace the damaged elements. All of this convoluted legalese is created to offer the underinsured two alternatives, neither of which is the full cost to repair or replace the damaged property element. The first alternative is the cost to repair, less the applicable depreciation. The second is the cost to repair after application of the deductible, less a reduction equal to the percentage by which the amount of insurance fails to satisfy the 80% replacement cost of the dwelling

Actual Cash Value and Replacement Cost

The dreaded term, *actual cash value,* continues to be defined in a variety of ways by insurers, statutes and judicial decisions. It is one of the most vexatious phrases found in any contract and more so because the homeowners policy makes no attempt to define it. One company employs the market value test while another will use replacement cost less depreciation. Others will include both of these methods in addition to any other factors that have a bearing on the property's value such as obsolescence and lack of utility. This method has come to be known as_*the broad evidence rule.* With respect to articles such as collectibles and fine arts that have never been appraised, none of these tests can resolve the question and, if they have any serious monetary value, they are a dispute waiting to happen. If there is a covered loss for such items, you can be assured that the insurer will challenge the value that is claimed by the insured right up until the final gavel strikes in the courtroom.

If you own a collection of ancient comic books, a numismatic or coin collection, a large selection of old "Life" or "Look" magazines, a pencil sketch by Wyeth or anything else of significant value, get them appraised and carefully photographed.

The valuation problem along with low limits on other classes of personal property like jewelry and silverware make a very strong argument in favor of scheduling or specifically insuring these items. This will increase the cost of the policy to some extent, but the savings in the event of a loss will easily offset the premium charge. In addition to value clarification, the scheduled property endorsement covers additional perils that are not included in the basic policy. The coverage under this form covers risks of all types except those that are specifically excluded. For example, a valuable stone is lost from its setting or you drop and break an expensive camera. They are both covered losses. The few exclusions in the form are relatively harmless

Actual cash value with respect to building losses is no less problematic. Adjusters usually make this calculation based upon the useful life expectancy of the element that is damaged. For example, if your home has a roof with a 20 year useful life and is 5 years old at the time of loss, it is probable that the company will pay only 75% of the cost to replace it deducting 25% for depreciation. Paint, wallpaper and other decorations have a much shorter life span, therefore greater depreciation. Make it clear (preferably in writing) with the company or its agent that you wish to comply with the replacement cost condition by obtaining sufficient coverage on your home.

When the adjuster or contractor inspects the damage to your home and prepares an estimate of the cost to complete repairs it is very important that you reach an agreement on both the repair cost and the scope of damage. If only one side of your roof or exterior walls are damaged, it is likely that the estimate will contemplate only repairs to the damaged area. It is also likely that the newly repaired area will not match the existing surface, and you are not compelled to accept a multi colored roof or mismatched siding. The same thing applies to carpeting and interior decorations. You are entitled to have your home restored to its pre loss condition.

Theft Coverage and Conditions

No one keeps receipts ad infinitum for property that has been purchased over a period of years or, in most cases, even months, but the fact remains that you must bear the burden of proving your claim. With respect to expensive items such as cameras and jewelry, the adjuster will ask where they came from, whether they were paid for by cash or credit, how long you have had them or if they were gifts, the name and address of the person who gave them to you. If you still have them, you may be asked to provide copies of owners' manuals, containers, or other material that accompanied the article in question.

It is a further condition of the policy that you report the theft to the police. Almost everyone knows that making a false police report is a crime and opens the theft claim to official investigation, creating a further deterrent to fraud.

All of these questions and the police involvement are designed to lessen the probability of fraud in the presentation of theft claims, however your inability to provide answers or documentation does not, in and of itself, constitute a basis for denial of your claim. In order to collect replacement cost on property that they do not wish to replace, some people make the purchase, get a receipt and return the item to the store at a later date. This might not be considered an act of fraud, but it is a shady practice and not one that is above reproach. Also on rare occasions, some homeowners discover lost valuables months or years after settlement of their claim, explaining that they had just misplaced the item in question. Some simply surrendered the property while others repaid the money. Is it possible that otherwise honest people simply made themselves a loan by reporting a theft that did not actually take place?

The reader should also keep in mind that, in most states, the stolen or damaged property must be replaced or repaired within 180 days or there will be no reimbursement beyond actual cash value. At least one State, however, has enacted legislation requiring companies to settle both personal property and building claims on a replacement cost basis without the replacement requirement. This flies in the face of the principle of indemnity, but state law supersedes the policy language. The indemnity concept sets forth the underlying purpose of insurance, that is to compensate the insured for loss, not to bestow a windfall profit, but there is no definition to be found anywhere in the property policy for actual cash value, making this the subject of litigation in many states.

Special Limits

While the homeowners policy covers your personal property, some items are subject to limited amounts and others are specifically excluded from coverage altogether.

Most people own many such articles, especially jewelry and silverware, with values greater than the limited coverage available in the basic homeowners forms; however the coverage for all of this property can be increased by purchasing, for an additional premium, what is known as a Scheduled Property or Personal Property Floater. In the case of particularly valuable items, it is possible that the insurer will require appraisals.

In general, the limits with which you should be concerned are those that are limited to loss by theft of jewelry ($1,000.00), firearms ($2000.00), and silverware ($2,500.00). There is a $200.00 limit on cash, $1,000.00 on securities, $1,000.00 on watercraft, $1,000.00 on trailers, $250.00 on property used in a business away from the residence premises. The latter would ordinarily apply to the tools used by repair people, mechanics or technicians in their trade. If you own valuable equipment of this type, carry it to job sites in your vehicle, then, by all means, you should inform your agent or company sales representative, and see that it is properly covered.

Fine arts and antiques are covered up to the limit of the policy's coverage for unscheduled personal property, but this class of property along with collectibles should be carefully documented, appraised and photographed. A careful scrutiny of their value by the adjuster may be expected at the time of loss.

Water Damage

There are a number of controversial chicken and egg issues surrounding the coverage and exclusions in connection with water damage. Following the devastation created by the hurricanes in 2004, there has been much publicity concerning the failure of the insurance industry to respond appropriately to victims of these storms. All homeowner's policies exclude flood and surface water damage, and it is based on this exclusion that most of these claims have been denied.

Hurricanes are almost always accompanied by a storm surge in which a dome of water at sea builds and spills onto the adjacent shore with rampaging force. This so-called wave wash, in combination with hurricane force winds, usually results in the total destruction of homes and other buildings within a short distance from the beach. Damage from the wind driven water is not covered, but there is coverage from any wind damage that precedes the wave wash. Since many of these homes simply disappear as they are wiped from their foundations, it is difficult, if not impossible, to establish the nature and extent of wind damage. Insurers are accused of applying improper influence on engineers engaged by them to make this determination, and this has resulted in many lawsuits with mixed results.

Coverage for flood and surface water, including that associated with storm surge, is available through the National Flood Insurance Program which is underwritten by the United States Federal Government. The insurance available under this program is limited to $250,000 on buildings and $100,000 on personal property. Anyone living in a flood zone or near an ocean beach will be required by their mortgage company to purchase flood coverage up to the amount of the mortgage or the available limit. All losses are subject to a deductible selected by the homeowner at the time the coverage is purchased. The standard form provides coverage on an actual cash value basis, but replacement cost is an option for an additional premium.

Another source of contention arises from the rupture and leakage of pipes and plumbing apparatuses. Some homeowners forms exclude damage resulting from "Repeated seepage or leakage of water or steam from within a plumbing, heating, air conditioning or automatic fire protective sprinkler system or from within an appliance for heating water or from within a household appliance which occurs over a period of weeks, months or years." The question arises as to how much of the damage took place when the leak began. The wording of this exclusion does not appear to rule out the initial damage. Also, coverage is extended to include the cost of tearing out and replacing any part of the building necessary to repair the system or appliance from which the leak originates.

If there has been extensive saturation of walls, ceilings or floors within your home, it is likely that insulation between the interior and exterior walls has absorbed some of the moisture. Unless the insulation is removed and replaced, there is a strong possibility that there could be a dangerous mold development. This is an issue that you should address with the adjuster or contractor at the time they assess the damage to your home.

Renters and Condominium Unit Owners Coverage

When you purchase a condominium unit, you are essentially buying the space contained within the interior walls, often described as a box of air, and an undivided interest in the building itself, the common areas and the land on which it is situated. What you have purchased is usually spelled out in the Declaration of Condominium and normally includes interior wall, floor and ceiling covers, as well as fixtures such as non-load bearing walls, cabinets, appliances and plumbing and electrical fixtures.

Unit owners' insurance is written on ISO form HO-6 called Condo owners. The policy covers your personal property, your personal liability, interior wall and floor coverings, interior cabinets and fixtures that do not constitute common elements, and improvements and upgrades that you have made. The building itself is covered by the association's master policy; so there is no coverage under HO-6 for the building and common areas. All of the other terms and conditions of the policy are the same as those found in the homeowner's policy.

Duties of the Insured after Loss

Almost all of the original provisions of the New York Standard Fire Insurance Policy's "165" lines have been included in the modern homeowners and commercial property policies. The text included in these "165" lines covers most of the important provisions of the policy including those dealing with exclusions, concealment and fraud and the insured's duties following a loss. One of the most important of these provisions concerns the requirement that the insured submit to examination under oath. This condition is used frequently in cases of suspected fraud and arson, and the Fifth Amendment prohibition against self-incrimination does not apply since there is no arrest or filing of criminal charges. Any material false swearing in the course of one or more of these examinations conducted by the insurer can constitute grounds for denial of the claim in its entirety. Questions framed in the examinations most often relate to motive and opportunity, requiring the insured to provide details concerning income, debt and general living circumstances. If the claim in question involves suspected arson, some of the questions will likely be:

Has there been an effort to sell the property? Has there been any change in family relationships; divorce, separation, etc.? Has anything taken place in the neighborhood that made the home less desirable? Have there been any previous claims, criminal convictions, lawsuits or bankruptcies? Has there been any change in the insured's employment status?

Deliberate misrepresentation in answering any of these questions gives rise to a possible denial, and becomes a potentially damning piece of evidence in a lawsuit against the insurer. The false swearing must be material to the coverage and claim in question, and the question of materiality is an issue that must be answered by the court. In the course of the litigation, it is likely that the insurer will demand copies of employment, tax and bank records to establish the insured's truthfulness or lack thereof concerning answers given regarding income and other financial matters. Courts have ruled that these records are relevant and must be produced. Lying under oath on these or any other question is extremely dangerous and should be avoided at all costs. You may be completely innocent of any fraudulent conduct, but deceptive answers just might turn a jury in the other direction.

This section also contains the requirement that you take reasonable measures to protect the property from further damage following a loss. If a covered peril such as wind or fire has created an opening in your roof or walls, then it is your responsibility to prevent additional water damage by covering the openings to the best of your ability.

Proving Your Loss

It is your responsibility, as the insured, to prove your loss. In a form called Sworn Statement in Proof of Loss, you will be required to answer the following questions:

- Amount of policy
- Dates of inception and expiration
- Policy number
- Location an d name of agent
- Full name of insured
- Perils insured against
- Date. time, cause and origin of loss
- Occupancy of the building
- Title and interest in the insured property
- Any changes since the policy was issued, such as occupancy, assignment of interest, possession location or exposure of the property described
- Value of the property
- Amount of loss and damage
- Amount claimed

With respect to personal property it is very important to maintain a thorough inventory accompanied by pictures. Some time when you have nothing better to do, walk around each room in your house, open drawers, cabinets and closets. Try to visualize every object contained within these rooms including the garage, basement, attic and any outbuildings. It almost never occurs to anyone that every single article down to pens and pencils or boxes of paper clips has a replacement cost or an actual cash value. Individually the value of such items may be inconsequential, but from a cumulative standpoint, they could represent a substantial sum. As I write this, I am looking at more than thirty assorted items on the top of my computer desk. To replace all of them would likely require several hundred dollars, excluding the computer itself. The items are nothing more than small office equipment, eye glasses, scissors, letter openers, trays, a lamp, tape dispenser, calculator, cell phone, pens and pencils. It is highly unlikely that without a thorough inventory I would remember these items if my house were to be completely destroyed.

Receipts, cancelled checks and billing statements are helpful in determining values, but they are not mandatory, and in the event of a catastrophic loss, it is likely that they would disappear or be destroyed unless they were placed in a safe deposit box off premises. Retail merchants who sell the personal property listed on the inventory are your best sources for determining the property's replacement cost.

The insurer will use a restoration contractor with whom they have established a relationship to assess the damage to your home and estimate the cost to repair or replace it. You can be reasonably assured that these contractors will use standard pricing for their work and will cut every possible corner to produce the lowest possible estimate. If your home is custom built, it may contain materials and decorations that are superior to those contemplated in computerized estimating programs used by adjusters and restoration contractors. You are entitled to repair and replacement with like kind and quality, so you should be certain that the final estimate takes this into consideration.

You should be aware that most of the contractors who maintain regular relationships with insurance companies, have few direct employees. Sub-contractors usually do the actual work. It is imperative that you determine that they are licensed, insured, have a reputation for quality workmanship and overall performance.

In order to avoid the assumption of responsibility for shoddy repair work, or dangerous defects, it is likely that your insurer will distance itself from the contract between you and the restoration contractor. Be careful what you sign. Beware of those good hands, good friends and good neighbors. They are not always on your side.

Frederick Staten

Pre Loss Inventory of Personal Property

1.Insert a floor plan sketch of your home showing location of major items of furniture.
2.Prepare a detailed inventory of personal property in categories as follows:

A. Furniture
B. Men's clothing
C. Women's clothing
D. Children's clothing
E. Kitchen appliances, cookware and utensils
F. China, crystal and silverware*
G. Jewelry*
H. Sports equipment, golf clubs, etc*
I. Computers and peripherals,
J. Office and desk supplies
K. Books
L. Paintings, wall hangings,
M. Figurines, statuary and other decorations
N. Tools, contents of base ment and garage
O. Lawn and garden equipment
P. Guns and ammunition *

*3.Consider insuring these items with a scheduled property floater since the standard policy provides limited coverage.
4. Photograph as much of the personal property as possible and include the pictures or a CD containing the pictures in your booklet.

Infrequently Reported
Homeowners Claims

Two obscure elements of coverage afforded by the homeowners' package are found in Section II, and while they do not cover the dwelling or personal property of the insured, they do not constitute protection from liability claims or lawsuits.

First there is medical payments, usually written with a $1,000.00 limit of liability. This coverage will pay the medical expenses incurred by any non resident who suffers an accidental injury while on the insured premises with the insured's permission, or is caused by the activities of an insured. For instance, your child or children are engaged in vigorous play on your premises with friends when one of them trips, falls and suffers a deep laceration or broken bone that requires emergency medical treatment.

One of your friends is helping you lift a heavy object when he drops it injuring one of his limbs or he simply suffers a serious back strain. These accidents do not normally impose any legal responsibility on your part, but your homeowners policy will pay the injured party's medical expenses up to the limit of liability.

While it does not involve a lot of money, there is also a coverage found in Section II of the Homeowners policy for *physical damage to property of others*. Most homeowners are not aware of the broad range of claims covered under this provision. The coverage is not widely publicized, and many claims that could be paid are presented only on rare occasions. The limit in the standard homeowners form is typically either $500.00 or $1,000.00.

This is sometimes called *goodwill coverage or voluntary property damage*. For example, you borrow a lawn mower from your neighbor, and it is damaged while in your possession. The cost to repair the mower is $350.00. You may or may not be legally liable for the damage, but for the purpose of this coverage, it doesn't matter. Your homeowners policy will pay the cost to repair or replace the property up to the specified limit in the policy. You are visiting the home of a friend, relative or neighbor. During a rare moment of clumsiness, you or a member of your family inadvertently bump into and knock over an expensive artifact, and it shatters into a thousand pieces. You spill a glass of red wine on an immaculate white carpet. You are shopping in an antique store, knock over a fragile article and break it. All of these examples are covered without the application of a deductible. The limit of liability may not be enough to cover the value or cost to repair the damage, but it will at least partially reimburse the owner.

Consider the thousands of homes located in golf communities and positioned in proximity to fairways where they are susceptible to repeated and frequent errant ball strikes. Roofs, windows, and screens are often damaged. Such damage is subject to the deductible in the owner of the home's insurance coverage, and the golfer is usually not legally responsible for the damage. The damage in individual incidents is relatively small, but some roofing contractors impose a minimum charge of several hundred dollars for a service call to replace a broken tile. Screens around enclosed porches and insulated thermal windows can be expensive to replace. Most of the time, the home owner is simply left to pay for the damage as the mishap goes unreported by the golfer to his insurance carrier. This is another example of a typical covered loss in the *physical damage to property of others endorsement* that is most often overlooked. Every golf community where this condition exists should notify its membership that they should utilize this coverage to reimburse their fellow members for such damage. These incidents seldom involve much money on an individual basis, but collectively, they represent millions in uncollected claims.

If your home is all or in part rendered uninhabitable to the extent that you and your family are unable to maintain your normal standard of living, then you are entitled to reimbursement for any additional living expenses that you incur. The damage could be confined to the kitchen, making the preparation of meals impossible. In such a case, you might choose to continue living in your home while the restoration is taking place, but this would necessitate eating in restaurants until the kitchen is restored. Carefully retain copies of restaurant checks paid during this period. This coverage is normally written with a limit of liability equal to 30% of the coverage on the insured dwelling. Should it become necessary for you to relocate temporarily, then you are entitled to reimbursement for the rental of a comparable residence until your home has been restored or you have permanently relocated. You do not have to accept an inferior living arrangement to accommodate the insurance company.

Almost every year, the western states suffer a rash of wildfires that destroy many homes and force the owners of others to evacuate. In order to preserve as much of their personal property as possible, many of these threatened homeowners hire movers and others to assist with the removal of their household goods, valuable paintings and objects of art to place them in storage for safekeeping until the fire threat is removed. Since fire is a covered peril, the cost of such removal and temporary storage is covered.

These provisions of the homeowners' policy are overlooked by thousands of policyholders who quietly accept the losses for which they could be reimbursed. Many consumers refrain from the presentation of these claims in fear of their company's cancellation or non renewal, and, to some extent their apprehension is justified.

Responsibility of the Agent
in the Claims Process

Insurance companies market their products through a variety of resources. Companies like Geico and a few others sell through mail and call centers. Others, such as State Farm and Nationwide, employ captive agents who are paid by commission but are not permitted to represent other companies. Then there are the independent agents who usually do represent more than one company and are also compensated by commission. Major industrial and commercial accounts are most often sold through large brokerage or risk management firms due to the complexity of coverage involved. Brokers can be held accountable for the selection of appropriate and sufficient coverage for a client whereas the independent agent has lesser duties to the insured customer and operates under the provisions and constraints of contracts with his companies.

The primary role of agents in the claims process is to accept reports from the insured and to give prompt notice of the accident or occurrence to the insurer. Some agents are afforded limited settlement authority, but this authority almost never includes the settlement of personal injury claims.

Agents who produce large premium volumes for a company often exercise substantial influence over the outcome of borderline coverage issues. This can add pressure on the adjuster as he attempts to comply with the policy's terms, creating a potential for inconsistency in the claims process. Some claims have been paid for so called business reasons , overlooking legitimate exclusions.

In addition to regular commissions paid to an agent for a particular line of business there is usually an additional sum that is variously called a contingent commission or profit sharing agreement. This can represent a substantial part of an agency's income, depending upon the profitability of the agent's entire book of business. In this sense, the agent has a vital interest in the reserves established and claims paid on behalf of his insured customers. This often causes disputes by agents who may believe loss reserves are overstated. Some companies, therefore, do not disclose reserves to their agents until the final computation of contingent commissions.

The agent, whether captive or independent, usually possesses adequate knowledge to recommend appropriate coverage to satisfy the consumer's needs. Careful consideration should be given to liability limits in auto and homeowner's policies with a particular emphasis on uninsured and under insured motorist coverage in the auto policy. Special situations, like business activities carried out from home, should be discussed with the agent. If the home is likely to be vacant or unoccupied for any period of time, this information must be provided to the insurer since the policy places limits on vacant and unoccupied property. Business property such as tools and equipment pertaining to a trade or profession require special coverage when they are off premises.

Commercial Property Claims

There is almost no limit to the variety of coverages that are available to the small and large business owner. Again, like the homeowners, these policies are usually packaged with Section I covering buildings, personal property, merchandise, manufactured goods, raw materials and machinery. They also include optional coverage for loss of profits due to business interruption and any necessary extra expense for the resumption of the business enterprise following a covered loss. Section II covers the business for its liability exposures that arise from its premises, operations and products.

The standard Business Owners' Policy (BOP) is usually written for the small business owner. It covers the insured building or any improvements and betterments that have been installed by the business owner, as well as merchandise and personal property used in the business. Most of the time, these policies are written in the broad form, covering all risks of physical damage except those that are specifically excluded. They can be tailored by endorsement to cover fluctuating inventories, multiple locations and other special risks. The insured business can select from a range of deductibles. Like the homeowners' policy, there is no coverage for flood or surface water, and there is no coverage under Section II for professional liability. If these exposures exist for a particular business or profession, then coverage for them must be purchased as separate policies.

Most business owners policies (BOP) include coverage for lost income and extra expense, resulting from a covered loss. The coverage for business income is generally limited to one year from the date of loss. Extra expense covers the additional costs to continue operations such as rental of alternate space or equipment and continuing payroll for key employees.

The commercial property policy is usually selected to cover large businesses such as major retail outlets, manufacturing risks, country clubs, hotels, resorts, contractors and many others. This policy is normally written, like the BOP, as a package consisting of up to ten coverage parts, providing substantial flexibility for modification to fit the needs of a particular enterprise. Time element coverages are also available as part of the package.

When a major commercial loss occurs, it is likely that the claim will be assigned to a heavily experienced adjuster, maybe even one who specializes in losses within the involved business. It is likely that the adjuster will engage the services of an accountant and a salvor to assist with the determination of value and loss sustained. The insured will be asked to provide a profit and loss statement, tax records and most recent inventories, sales and production records along with names and addresses of suppliers. Engineers and other specialists may be engaged to provide input concerning the necessity for incurring extra expense and projecting reasonable estimates of restoration time.

Almost all commercial policies include a co-insurance clause, which is a rate reduction device. The insured will be required to purchase coverage equal to a percentage (often 80%) of value of the insured property. For example if the property involved has a value of $1,000,000, the required amount of insurance would be $800,000. If the insured purchases only $400,000, the business will suffer a 50% co-insurance penalty on any partial loss; so a loss in amount of $400,000 would result in a payment of only $200,000.

Business income and extra expense coverage is available as an optional coverage under the commercial package policy and is also offered with various co-insurance applications. Like all time element policies, the business income endorsement covers net income and normal operating expenses including payroll during a period of suspension due to a loss covered by one of the insured perils. In the application for insurance, the insured will provide actual earnings for the previous 12 months and an estimate for the next 12 months, taking into consideration projected sales and expenses based upon current trends. It is based upon these calculations that the limit of insurance is established as well as the co-insurance percentage. In the case of large retail and manufacturing risks, this can be an extremely complicated accounting process with extensive participation by the insured's financial and accounting personnel. The insurance limit must also take into consideration the estimated time that would be required to complete restoration following a loss.

In major losses there are often salvageable goods with little or no obvious damage. The salvor, employed by the adjuster, will separate the damaged from the undamaged items, conduct a total physical inventory and arrange for storage and disposition of the salvaged items. Such materials are either sold at a reduced wholesale price or left with the insured for an agreed sum to reduce the loss payment.

If the loss is substantial and complex, the insurer will engage the services of a forensic accountant who will do a thorough analysis of all the financial aspects of the insured business. In order to establish a projection of profit or loss, the accountant will examine books, tax records, gross sales and purchases of goods or raw materials.

The determination of value and loss, coverage for questionable items and other relevant matters can be extremely time consuming, costly and laborious; so it is not uncommon for a business to engage the services of a public adjusting service. Public adjusters are never employed by the insurer. Their service is provided exclusively to the insured in determining the amount of covered loss and negotiating settlement with the insurer's adjuster. Most of the time these people are experts in the business of property loss adjusting, and they are frequently able to provide the insured with a more favorable result than might otherwise have been achieved. In addition to the negotiation of the best settlement possible, the public adjuster can make sure that the insured complies with all of the policy's terms and conditions.

Many public adjusters are former company employees. They are regulated by the state in which their business is domiciled and must pass a comprehensive licensing exam. Their work comes very close to the practice of law; however, it is granted exception from the unlawful practice by legislative enactment. Fees are charged on a contingent basis, usually for up to 10% of the amount recovered.

Commercial Crime Losses

Every business and public institution has an exposure to financial loss due to robbery, burglary, employee theft or embezzlement. The industry provides a myriad of forms that can be tailored to suit the requirements of a particular enterprise. Employee dishonesty is covered under an instrument called a *blanket bond*. While this coverage is a bond other than insurance, it is written to guarantee the honest performance of an organization's employees, especially those who are in a position to handle financial transactions and in house accounting. Through concealed manipulation of accounts, there have been innumerable cases involving huge sums resulting from embezzlement by trusted employees over a period of months or even years .Under this coverage which can be included in the Commercial Insurance Package, the employer will be reimbursed for losses sustained. There is , however, an exclusion for losses that must be proven only by inventory shortage. While such shortages may be used as evidence of loss, there must also be another source to prove that the loss resulted from employee dishonesty.

The Catastrophe Dilemma

All areas of the United States are prone to a disaster of one kind or another. The west is subject to the annual outbreak of wildfires and occasionally gets a double whammy with earthquakes. The plains states are devastated by tornadoes, flooding and blizzards. The gulf, south and Atlantic coasts are beset with hurricanes of varying intensity.

Some of the destruction brought about by these events is covered by existing insurance policies, but much of it is either excluded or priced beyond the reach of the average property owner. Most of the property-casualty companies currently doing business in the country rely on their reinsurance contracts to provide themselves with the financial capacity to weather these storms, but none of them, individually or collectively, have addressed the issue of closing gaps and reducing costs of catastrophe coverage.

Because of their long-term history of profitability, it should be incumbent upon them to devise a workable solution to the problem. It should not be the responsibility of government or the public at large to formulate the plan.

There is no Federal regulation of the insurance industry, but if there was, the companies could be compelled to incorporate disaster coverage into their policies on a national basis, and the law of large numbers would reduce the cost to the individual policyholder. There would be some opposition to this type of plan from the residents of states that are less exposed to one or more of these perils, but sharing of risk is fundamental to the insurance process. Regrettably, competition and greed among the carriers will be a continuing detriment to a plan of this kind unless it can be shown that such a plan will increase the profit levels of the industry.

Outside the catastrophe coverage, the underlying policies would be unchanged with respect to covered perils, except none of these perils would be covered if the loss arises from a catastrophe that is designated and has a number assigned by the Insurance Service Office. This designation would trigger coverage under the catastrophe plan for all losses caused by the disaster, i.e.; fire, wind, flood, etc. A similar arrangement now exists between primary companies and their re-insurers.

The substitution of coverage from the underlying contracts to an all inclusive disaster peril would reduce the exposure under the basic policies to a level in which rates could be dramatically lower for all homeowners and commercial property policies. This plan could be merged with the National Flood Insurance program, enabling the transfer of the funds from that program to a reinsurance subsidy with which to offset a portion of the costs for the new plan.

At the time this is written, the industry has been free from major hurricane losses for more than 5 years. During that time, had all the property insurance companies cooperated to form a national disaster insurance program, there would now be a substantial surplus to pay the losses from the next storm that is sure to come.

Reinsurance

Unseen but looming in the background is a giant segment of the industry called *reinsurance*. It may surprise you to learn that insurance companies insure themselves against loss by purchasing contracts from other companies who share in the claims made against the underlying company. The amount of coverage provided by a reinsurance company depends upon the type of risk assumed, the size of the underlying carrier and its financial capacity to sustain losses.

In some respects, reinsurance transactions bear a striking similarity to the process in which bookmakers *lay off* a portion of bets to be certain that they will have the resources to pay a successful wager for an unanticipated result.

There are both domestic and international reinsurance companies, and many primary carriers also participate in the reinsurance market through a risk sharing process.

Every claim that is reported finds its way into the books of a reinsurer in one way or another, since the overall loss experience of an underlying company has a direct bearing on the rate charged for its reinsurance contracts. Therefore, the establishment of reserves on individual claims is closely watched by the reinsurance carrier, and in some cases, it will create its own reserve that exceeds that of the primary carrier. The claims departments of reinsurance companies tread very cautiously in this area to avoid being included as an additional defendant in cases that might involve bad faith on the part of the primary carrier. While they might make recommendations for disposition of a serious claim, they will do so very quietly with a low profile and never in writing.

Reinsurance agreements frequently afford the reinsurer the right to periodically review individual claim files. These reviews focus on the quality of claims handling and the overall accuracy of reserves. Their findings can impact the evaluation of the primary carrier's claim personnel from top to bottom.

The cost of reinsurance is reflected in the rates charged to the consumer for every line of insurance, and for this reason, the reinsurance industry represents a decisive factor in the provision of insurance throughout the world. Without it, most primary carriers would not have sufficient capacity to accept the risks that they now take.

Two Bizarre Homeowners' Claims

> The stories that follow are included to demonstrate just how imaginative the legal system can be in asserting insurance coverage for exotic situations.

AN ACCIDENTAL MURDER

Jack Ward finished his last service call for the day almost two hours ahead of schedule; so instead of returning to the shop, he decided to go home. When he arrived at the house, he noticed a police cruiser parked in his driveway. His wife worked as a crossing guard for the city under the authority of the police department, and while the presence of the police vehicle was unusual, there were occasions when one of the officers would give her a ride home.

Jack entered the house through the unlocked front door that opened directly into the living room of the small two bedroom bungalow. He saw no one but heard some noise coming from the master bedroom down the hall toward the rear of the house. He quietly walked down the hallway and opened the bedroom door which was slightly ajar. He was stunned to a point of shock by what he saw. His wife, Mary, and her police sergeant supervisor were engaged in vigorous sexual intercourse.

"What in Hell is going on?" He exclaimed. "I can't believe this!"

As the pair of lovers separated in startled surprise, Jack noticed that the sergeant had left his clothing and his service revolver on a chair near the doorway. As the couple repositioned themselves in bed, Jack withdrew the weapon from its holster and pointed it in their direction. Delirious with rage, he screamed, "How long has this shit been going on?"

Mary came back with a weak, tear laden response, "I'm sorry, Jack; it just happened. This is the first time, I swear it. Please, I'm sorry."

The sergeant shrugged his shoulders with a guilt ridden smirk on his face and started to say, "Jack, you ought to put the gun ---", but before he could finish, there was an explosion that reverberated through the house as the heavy .357 magnum discharged. The bullet entered the sergeants forehead and exited through the back of his skull, taking with it a huge section of brain matter and bone fragments. The young police officer was instantly transformed into a wide eyed corpse. Mary screamed, rolled out of the bed and ran, panic stricken, into the living room where she collapsed.

Without saying a word, Jack threw the gun on the bedroom floor and left the house, barely glancing at Mary who had assumed a fetal position on the living room floor and continued to shriek at the top of her voice.

Jack drove his small van with no destination in mind. His thoughts were disorganized as he struggled to decide what to do next, He knew, beyond any doubt, that he would very soon become the subject of an intensive manhunt. "I killed a cop," he thought, "one of their own! I'll be public enemy number one. They won't care why I did it. They'll kill me without even trying to make an arrest. What in the name of God has happened to me?" Thoughts about the sequence of events raced through his mind like subliminal images, and he convinced himself that pulling the trigger was an involuntary muscle reaction, that he never intended to fire the gun or kill his wife's lover.

Within less than an hour of confused meandering, Jack finally decided that he had no alternative but to surrender himself. He drove to the nearest police station. Visibly shaken, he went inside and spoke with the officer on duty at the entrance. "My name is Jack Ward," he said. "I accidentally shot Sergeant Paul Wells. It was not intentional; it was an accident. I know how it looks, but it was an accident."

By this time, Mary had recovered sufficiently from her initial shockto call the emergency medical service, and upon their discovery of the lifeless victim they notified the police. A search for Jack was already under way. The officer at the desk looked up quickly and said, "Yeh, we know about it. We're looking for you. Turn around, put your hands behind your back. You're under arrest for the murder of Sergeant Paul Wells." With that he placed handcuffs on Jack's wrists and carefully informed him of his rights. Next he was taken to a holding cell where he was told that he would be held pending his arraignment.

In the weeks and months that followed, Jack was indicted and went to trial on a charge of second degree homicide. To everyone's astonishment, the jury was either incredibly sympathetic or chose to believe Jack's contention that the shooting was accidental. In any event, he was acquitted.

Understandably, the reader of this story will ask, "What is the connection of a passion killing to homeowners' insurance coverage?"

While the criminal trial was pending, Sergeant Wells' widow filed a civil suit against Jack in which both intentional infliction of harm and negligence were alleged in the declaration. The appellate courts in the state where the incident occurred had already ruled that if a lawsuit contained a count of negligence, then that alone would trigger the coverage for defense under a liability insurance policy, including the liability coverage under Section II of the Homeowners policy. The company for whom I was employed wrote the homeowners coverage for Jack Ward, so that put us squarely in the middle of this appalling story.

After Jack was acquitted, he left the state and his new address was unknown. I questioned relatives, friends and former employers to no avail; so I employed a private investigator who was noted for his expertise in skip tracing. Inside a month, he located Jack, living with a young woman and working as an air conditioning mechanic in Miami, Florida. The neighborhood where his address was located was in North Miami off the beach. The houses were small multiplex units in what could best be described as a low rent development with mixed ethnicity occupants. It was not considered dangerous ---in the daytime, but there was moderate drug activity, and it was not the kind of place where ordinary citizens ventured after dark.

Our defense council was of the opinion that the only way we could prevail in the lawsuit was to have Jack testify in the civil case as he did in the criminal proceedings. Even then, it was less than a 50-50 chance that a civil jury would be as sympathetic as the one that acquitted him. It became apparent that I would have to persuade Jack to return for the trial and take the stand on his own behalf. Under the policy conditions, he was obligated to cooperate , but considering the utter destruction of his life as he knew it, he would not be seriously concerned about a judgment whether it was paid by his insurance company or not. If he refused to testify, we might find grounds to deny coverage, but only if we could show that our defense was prejudiced by his failure to appear.

Within a couple of days of learning where he was, I boarded a plane for Miami. Arriving late in the evening, I rented a car and checked into a hotel for the night. The next morning, I drove to the address which the detective had learned was Jack's home. There were no vehicles parked in the driveway or on the street in front of the house; so I assumed that both Jack and his girlfriend were working. The neighborhood was quiet at this time, and the only people I saw were children waiting for school buses with their mothers.

I returned later in the day, after normal working hours, on the assumption that Jack would be home. When I knocked, a man who I assumed was our insured, came to the door. He was a nondescript Caucasian, about thirty years of age. I introduced myself and explained that, I wanted to discuss the pending lawsuit with him. With a grimace, he said, "I thought all of that crap was behind me. That's why I came down here. How did you find me?"

"I used a private investigator." I said. "I don't know anything about his methods for finding people, but he probably has connections with Social Security and state motor vehicle departments. Have you obtained a Florida driver's license?"

"Yeh, that's probably how he found me." he answered.

"Jack, in order to get rid of this case and prevent you from having a judgment against you, I need your help. First, I would like to ask you some questions and record your answers on my tape recorder. Next, I want to talk with you about returning to testify at the trial."

With obvious reluctance, he said, "Come on in. I'm only going to tell you what I told the court, and I'm sure as Hell not promising that I will go through another trial."

Jack agreed to the recording of his statement in which he related the events exactly as he had from the beginning, insisting that the weapon was discharged by an involuntary muscle reaction; that he had not intended to hurt anyone. He admitted that he was outraged beyond belief but added, "If I had meant to kill that guy, wouldn't I have shot them both?"

I was never able to get a firm commitment from him as to whether or not he would return to testify at the trial, and during the weeks that followed there were numerous motions, pleadings and pre-trial negotiations. Our policy limit was $100,000 and the defense costs were mounting with every legal maneuver. Ultimately, we were presented with a settlement offer that was much less than the limit to which we might have been exposed, and the case was settled. The motivation to settle was based upon simple economics, not contractual responsibility.

Homeowners' liability insurance never contemplated coverage for a claim like this, but the question as to whether or not the policyholder's act was intentional would have been left to a jury based upon his testimony that the gun was fired accidentally. As people who are familiar with guns know, a revolver is generally a *double action* weapon, meaning that it can be fired in two separate ways. One option , demanding more and is to draw the hammer back so the gun is *cocked* and requires only a very light pressure on the trigger. The other is simply to squeeze the trigger hard enough to draw back the hammer and release it to fire in a single movement of the trigger. The latter method requires a much more forceful trigger pressure.

Because the case was settled before it went to trial, there was no examination of the pistol by an expert to determine the amount of pressure to fire it without cocking, and Jack's testimony would be that he could not remember whether or not he cocked it. This seemed to be a convenient lapse of memory since cocking the gun would imply his intent to fire it. In any event, I was never convinced that the shooting was accidental, and in a staff meeting some time after the settlement, the case came under discussion, and one of our other officers made an attempt at humor by saying, "Maybe we should advertise that our homeowner's policy even covers you for murder."

1

HARRY AND JANE

If ever there was a "hail fellow well met", it was Harry whose surname will remain anonymous. With a large frame but not corpulent, he had an effervescent smile with lively sparkling eyes, deep set in a red face grown more generous by a receding hair line. He was a little over 70, retired comfortably from a government job that gave rise to extensive overseas tours that were mostly on the European continent. His one and only marriage, from which there were no children, went sour many years earlier. After that most of his relationships with members of the opposite sex, and there were many, were short term. As an alternative to companionship, Harry found comfort in relating stories about his work and travels to fellow patrons of a local bar where he spent many of his waking hours. Through his outgoing nature, he had a lot of friends, many of them women, but no serious relationships.

Then along came Jane, and life for old Harry was about to make a radical change. Jane was a diminutive widow of another government employee. At 75 she had a few wrinkles around the corner of her eyes, but her well proportioned body and her demeanor were not those of a super senior. She could easily have been mistaken for a 60 year old. Like Harry, she was gregarious, yet refined and possessed of a superb intellect. From the first time they met, it appeared that she and Harry were a complimentary match. Both were connoisseurs of books and the arts with a deep appreciation for elegant life styles. They lived in the same upscale high rise condominium , and they met at one of the association meetings.

In a short time they began to see one another almost daily, sharing fine dinners at expensive restaurants, all manner of entertainment in theatrical performances, lecture halls and museums. Inevitably, their mutual affection blossomed and the prospect of spending the balance of their lives together became a cherished idea. They continued to live apart due to the separate ownership of their condominium units, but there was a silent understanding between them that marriage was in their future. While there was no overpowering hormonal surge in their aging bodies, embers from old fires still smoldered and a sexual relationship was slowly awakened. In the absence of great passion, their love making was hesitant, brief and infrequent, more gesture than profound consummation.

In the meantime, Jane informed her family in a distant New England city that she had met someone, that they had a strong feelings for one another and might very well marry and spend the rest of their lives together. Her family, two adult children and a sister, were overjoyed and hastened to invite Jane to bring Harry to their homes where they could meet him. When Jane told Harry about her conversation, he readily agreed to travel with her for a visit.

The trip to New England went off without a hitch. They stayed at the home of Jane's oldest son and his wife, properly sleeping in separate rooms. Meeting people and mingling with strangers was second nature for Harry; and his open friendliness made it easy for him to be embraced as a welcome companion for Jane. She had been a widow for almost five years, and her loneliness was a matter of deep concern to her family who had been fearful that her next life stage would involve a nursing home or some other long term care facility.

On the way home, Jane casually commented on "how nice it would be if the two of them could find a place to live that was closer to her relatives." The remark penetrated Harry's soul like a bullet. He felt as though some lurking spirit had doused his spine with ice water. During the rest of the trip, there were long periods of silence, broken only when Jane attempted to initiate conversation. Harry struggled to avoid the appearance of sulking, but it was obvious that he was troubled. When Jane asked him about it, he answered that he " had a headache."

In the weeks that followed, Jane began to disclose more of her visions for their future together, demanding more and more of his time and attention to the point where Harry felt smothered. The bloom was clearly falling off the rose. Deep rooted habits were hard to break and the old man was becoming seriously conflicted about the loss of the absolute freedom he had enjoyed for so many years. He was neither responsible for nor accountable to any other person ,and, upon reflection, he could only envision a troubled road ahead.

Over the next few months, he started to make himself less available, went away for long weekends and returned to his neighborhood bar. Now, though, he was drinking more heavily, returning to his apartment in the evening less than sober but not in a drunken stupor.

Jane left messages on his answering service which he often ignored, and in the end , without bitterness, Harry's fervor simply cooled as it always had in past relationships. He was the kind of man that, despite his good qualities, could not sacrifice his lifelong independence.

A few weeks went by, and Jane awoke one morning, startled to discover that an angry rash had broken out inside and outside her vaginal orifice. She immediately called the office of her gynecologist and made an urgent appointment for the same day. As the female doctor, an old friend, was conducting her examination, Jane asked, "What in the Hell is it, Pat?" Without hesitation, the doctor replied, "Jane, dear girl, you have contracted a bad case of genital herpes. We can treat the symptoms and make you more comfortable, but the disease is incurable. It's episodic and will reoccur. Have you been sexually active recently? If you have, you should inform your partner that he has herpes and has given you a sexually transmitted disease. I'm so sorry Jane, I wish I could just give you a shot or a pill and make it go away, but it's one of those bugs that we have yet to conquer."

As she left the office, choking back tears, the doctors words pounded through Jane's mind like a jackhammer " incurable - episodic - genital herpes. How could this be happening?" she thought. "Damn you, Harry! Why didn't you tell me?"

The reason Harry didn't tell her was because he thought he was not contagious unless he was suffering an outbreak. He contracted genital herpes in Europe some years earlier, had a few minor episodes but his disease had been dormant for more than two years.

A few days later, after she recovered from the initial shock and feelings of rage, Jane tried to contact Harry by telephone and knocking on his apartment door. There was no response. She even went to his favorite bar and made inquiries only to learn that no one there had seen him for more than a week. Finally, in an act of desperation, she wrote a note and left it under his door. The note was a terse two lines that read

"Harry, we need to talk. You have given me genital herpes."

Harry found the note several days later when he returned from a visit with friends on the west coast. He read it, took a deep breath and said to himself, "Oh! Hell!" There and then, he decided that his best course of action was to do nothing. A face to face confrontation with Jane would only serve to further aggravate the problem's gravity.

The next several days were uneventful, then a letter appeared in Harry's mailbox that bore the return address of one of the nations most prominent law firms. In addition to the partners, there were at least a hundred associates, some of whom represented figures in the Watergate scandal. Preeminence is too mild a word to describe the reputation of this firm. If there was a weighty constitutional issue to be argued before the Supreme Court in which a corporation or prominent politician sought relief, there was a good possibility that one of the firm's super lawyers would argue the case.

The letter from an associate informed Harry that the firm had been retained by Jane to represent her in the matter of a personal injury inflicted upon her through Harry's negligent and willful misconduct.

There were no further details, but the writer suggested that Harry would be advised to retain counsel as a lawsuit against him was contemplated unless an appropriate settlement could be agreed upon.

Harry was alarmed by the threat from this Goliath among law firms, but on reflection, he did not believe Jane would expose her relationship with him in a lawsuit that was certain to generate a lot of notoriety. He didn't respond to the letter by calling Jane's attorney as instructed but did consult with his own attorney. After Harry related the story of broken romance between Jane and him, the lawyer asked, "Do you think she'll go through with it?"

"I don't know, she's mad as Hell; and I didn't handle our breakup very well. She's a tough old bird. She just might do it." Harry replied.

The lawyer chuckled a little, then for the first time, the specter of liability insurance reared its ugly head. Harry, do you have any kind of insurance that might protect you in this kind of lawsuit?"

Harry thought for a moment, and responded with, "I don't think so. I have a homeowners condominium policy, an automobile policy and an umbrella policy. I don't see how any of those would apply to this problem?"

Grinning, the attorney said, "It will certainly be a case of first impression, but I think we should take a look at the homeowner's policy and the umbrella policy. Bring your policies in, and we'll go over them."

This story took place at a time when the HIV epidemic was in its earliest stages, and the implications for insurance coverage to protect an insured from lawsuits arising from the transmission of communicable diseases were never considered. There was already an exclusion in most policies eliminating coverage for "intentional acts", but several courts had ruled that if the suit contained an allegation of negligence then the company must still provide a defense before resolving the coverage issue.

The next day, Harry brought his homeowner's and umbrella policies to the attorney and after a giving them a thorough review, he looked at Harry and said, "Harry, I don't see a thing in either of these policies that would preclude coverage for this potential lawsuit. It was an occurrence. It was not intentional and it did result in bodily injury for which you could potentially be liable. The only language that even comes close to permitting the company to deny coverage and refusing to defend is "bodily injury" or "property damage" which is expected or intended by the insured."

"Harry, you and Jane engaged in consensual sex, but you did not intentionally transmit this disease to Jane. You told me that your own infection has been dormant for more than 2 years and to the best of your knowledge and belief, you have never infected anyone else. Report this matter to your homeowner's carrier and tell them you expect them to provide a defense. Let me know how they respond."

Although it was embarrassing, Harry visited the office of his independent insurance agent, spoke with on of the owners and gave him a brief synopsis along with copies of the note from Jane and the letter from her attorney. The agent was skeptical but held back his impulse to laugh out loud and agreed to report the case to the homeowner's carrier. When he left , Harry imagined the outrageous comments and ribald humor that would run through the office when the report was shared with other members of the agent's staff. Had Harry and Jane been a couple in their twenties or thirties, there would have been some discussion about coverage for this bizarre event, but for two people in their 70s, it was looked upon as a comedy.

When the agent called, one of my assistants spoke with him and took the report. He brought it to me, laughing almost uncontrollably. He showed no sense of sympathy for either party and obviously considered the affair to be ludicrous.

When I looked at the sketchy facts, my immediate reaction was that there was no coverage , so I sent a *reservation of rights* letter accompanied by a *non waiver agreement* to Harry with a copy to his attorney and Jane's attorney. These were forms with boiler plate language, intended to preserve the future rights of both parties while the company conducted its investigation, standard practice in cases where coverage was questionable or at issue.

After the *non waiver agreement* was signed and returned to us, I arranged for a meeting with Harry in my office. I engaged the services of a court reporter and questioned Harry at length and under oath. He gave me the details precisely as they were related in the foregoing narrative. He admitted openly that he had been unfair in his relationship with Jane but emphatically denied that he ever had an outbreak of herpes during the time that they were together. He left me perplexed as to how I should respond to Jane's attorney. I had a brief conversation with him shortly after taking Harry's statement and simply told him that we were still in the process of completing our investigation. I asked him whether or not he would permit his client to give us a statement in his presence. Surprisingly he agreed, and said that he would talk with Jane to set up an appointment.

I went over the case in detail with our chief executive officer, the head of our underwriting department and others. Without exception, they all took the position that there was no coverage, citing the intentional act exclusion, not a "bodily injury" or the useless excuse that the policy was not intended to cover things like this. I explained the obvious contradictions, pointing out that in order to limit or eliminate coverage for a factual situation it was necessary to "say what you mean and mean what you say." The argument that a herpes infection did not constitute bodily injury bore a little more weight, but the policy did not offer a definition of bodily injury; so this would likely be a question to be resolved by a jury in a *declaratory judgment* suit, asking the court to define the term and render a decision on coverage.

There was no question in my mind that Harry's attorney would file such a suit if we refused to provide a defense to the underlying case sure to be filed by Jane. Furthermore there had been some decisions requiring the insurer to pay the fees of the insured's personal attorney in cases where coverage was being contested. The attorney engaged to represent the insured in the original case could not represent him on the coverage issue since it might well make him privy to information that would be a detriment to his client's assertion of coverage. This would constitute a flagrant conflict of interest. So it was entirely possible that our company might have to pay the fees for our own attorney in the underlying litigation, the insured's personal counsel on the coverage issue and a separate attorney on our behalf to prosecute or defend the potential *declaratory judgment* action.

Our company's agreements with its re-insurers required that we report all claims with a reserve in excess of a certain dollar amount, and because of the potential exposure to a large jury award plus the defense costs, I placed a reserve on the case that was in excess of our maximum retained limit (for all purpose and intents, a deductible amount payable by the company without re-insurance participation).

As the ramifications continued to pile up, it seemed that I had the entire industry looking over my shoulder with a lot of "Monday morning quarterbacking". Before we met with Jane and her attorney to get Jane's version of the facts and what she wanted to settle the matter, it occurred to me that the complexities of the case were growing to a point well beyond "my pay grade", and it was clear that I needed legal help before taking any further steps. Without further delay, I selected one of my favorite defense firms, a team of two young and talented professionals with whom I had successfully worked in the past. I Had already discussed the case with them on an informal basis, so when the day came for taking Jane's statement one of the partners accompanied me to the office of her attorney where he would conduct an informal examination under oath.

This statement which was, in reality, a deposition would not have been available without the consent of Jane and her attorney since the process of *discovery* would not commence until suit was filed and service of process was completed upon the defendant, Harry.

Discovery is the process in civil law that permits both parties to depose witnesses, call for the production of documents and generally examine evidence that is to be presented by the opposing party or parties.

When we were introduced, we found Jane to be very much as Harry had described her. She was pleasant, refined and articulate. Her answers, in the course of her questioning, were frank, not excessively verbose and were almost totally consistent with Harry's version of what took place. Although she still must have been teeming with pent up rage, there was no hysteria, no tearful outbursts, no sense of hatred or vengeance, yet in a quiet but firm way, she conveyed the idea that Harry's unconscionable behavior had caused her great harm that would shatter her few remaining years. I saw that she would make an extremely impressive witness before any jury, and the venue for this case was noted for its high awards. She would appear to most as someone's mother or grandmother who had been victimized by a sex crazed scoundrel.

Surprisingly, the initial demand for settlement was much less than I had anticipated, a mere $100,000. After some additional negotiation, an agreement was reached and the case was settled for slightly more than half of the original demand. Some of my associates still believed that there was no coverage for this claim under the homeowners' policy, but it is noteworthy that within a short time, the industry firmly closed the gap by creating a new exclusion in the standard form to preclude coverage for the transmission of sexually transmitted disease.

Appendices

I

Comparative negligence doctrines

The following four states and the District of Columbia are the only ones remaining that observe the contributory negligence doctrine, barring recovery for any degree of fault by the victim.

They are: Alabama, District of Columbia, Maryland, North Carolina and Virginia.

Thirteen states recognize the pure comparative fault rule, which allows a damaged party to recover even if such a party is 99% at fault, although the recovery is reduced by the damaged party's degree of fault.

The states that observe this rule are:

Alaska Missouri

Arizona New Mexico

California New York

Florida Rhode Island

Kentucky South Dakota

Louisiana Washington

Mississippi

The following twelve states follow the 50% bar rule, meaning a damaged party can only recover damages if he is 49% or less at fault.

Arkansas
Colorado
Georgia
Idaho
Kansas
Maine
Nebraska
North Dakota
Oklahoma
Tennessee
Utah
West Virginia

II

Unfair Insurance Practices Act

The following is an overview of the pertinent elements of the Model Unfair Insurance Practices Act:

1. Misrepresentation of pertinent facts or insurance policy provisions relating to coverage at issues.

2. Denial of a claim under a purportedly cancelled policy with knowledge that statutory cancellation procedures have not been followed.

3. Deliberate misrepresentation of legal precedent to avoid paying a claim.
   Filing a false material statement regarding a person's financial status or business.

4. Failing to acknowledge and act reasonably and promptly on communication with respect to pending claims.

5. An insurer should not necessarily delay payment of policy proceeds.

6. The Model Act suggests that every insurer should acknowledge receipt of a claim within ten (10) business days and respond to all pertinent communications from a claimant which reasonably requires a response.

7. The insurer should promptly provide the insured with necessary claims forms and reasonable assistance in complying with policy conditions.

8. The insurer must adopt and implement reasonable standards for prompt investigation of claims.

9. The insurer should conduct a thorough and adequate investigation of each claim.

10. The Model Act suggests that claim investigation should be completed within thirty (30) days after notification. If the investigation cannot be completed within that time, the insured should be kept apprised of the status. It should be noted the insurer cannot avoid a bad faith claim by failing to investigate, and thus avoiding acquisition of the facts to support the insured's claim.

11. An insurer cannot refuse to pay a claim without conducting a reasonable investigation based on all available information.

12. An insurer cannot unreasonably delay the investigation or resolution of a claim.

13. An insurer must make a good faith attempt to effectuate prompt, fair and equitable settlement of claims in which liability has become reasonably clear.

14. An insurer must not force an insured to institute litigation to recover amounts due under the insurance policy by offering substantially less than the amount ultimately recovered.

15. An insurer must not force an insured to initiate suit when no substantial defense exists.

16. An insurer must not attempt to settle a claim for less than full value based on information in the application that was included or added without the knowledge of the insured.

17. An insurer must not delay payment or settlement of a claim by requiring an insured to produce documentation of the claim, and then requiring a formal proof of loss, which contains the same information.

18. An insurer must not delay or refuse to settle a portion of a claim when liability is reasonably clear in order to influence settlement of other portions of the claim.

19. An insurer must not fail to tender the full amount the insurer believes is due and owing.

20. An insurer must promptly provide a reasonable explanation of the basis for the denial of a claim or for an offer to compromise.

21. An insurer must provide a proper defense.

22. An insurer must provide separate council for the insured when there is a conflict of interest.

23. An insurer must promptly and fully advise the insured of the danger of an excess verdict.

24. An insurer must negotiate in good faith.

25. An insurer must follow the advice of counsel unless there is reasonable justification to not do so.

26. An insurer must not ask an insured to contribute to any settlement that is within policy limits.

III

State Insurance Departments

The departments listed below each have an office toaddress consumer complaints regarding insurance issues of all kinds, including claims disputes.The chart also includes statuatory limits required for autmobile liability insurance.

ALABAMA DEPARTMENT of
INSURANCE
135 South Union Street #200
Montgomery, Alabama 36130
(334) 269-3550
Minimum Limits 20/40/10

ALASKA DIVISION of
INSURANCE
333 Willoughby Ave 9th Floor
Juneau, Alaska 99811-0805
(907) 465-2515
(907) 465-3422 (Fax)
Minimum Limits 50/100/25

ARIZONA DEPARTMENT of
INSURANCE
2910 North 44th Street #210
Phoenix, Arizona 85018
(800) 325-2548 (In State)
(602) 912-8444
Minimum Limits 15/30/10

ARKANSAS DEPARTMENT of
INSURANCE
1200 West 3rd Street
Little Rock, Arkansas 72201-1904
(501) 371-2600
Minimum Limits 25/50/15

CALIFORNIA DEPT. of
INSURANCE
300 Capital Mall # 1700
Sacramento, California 95814
(800) 927-HELP (In State)
(213) 897-8921
Minimum Limits 15/30/5

COLORADO DIVISION of
INSURANCE
1560 Broadway # 850
Denver, Colorado 80202
(303) 894-7499
Minimum Limits 25/50/15

DISTRICT OF COLUMBIA
DEPT. of INSURANCE
441 Fourth Street NW 8th Floor
Washington D.C. 20001
(202) 727-8000
Minimum Limits 25/50/10

FLORIDA DEPARTMENT of
INSURANCE
200 East Gaines St., Larson
Building
Tallahassee, FL 32399
Toll-free in state: (800) 342-2762
(850) 922-3100
Minimum Limits 10/20/10

GEORGIA INS. FIRE SAFETY
COMM.
2 Martin L. King Jr. Drive (704
West Tower)
Atlanta, Georgia 30334
(404) 656-2056
Minimum Limits 25/50/25

HAWAII INSURANCE
COMMISSIONER
250 South King Street 5th Floor
Honolulu, Hawaii 96813
(808) 586-2790
Minimum Limits 15/35/10

INDIANA DEPARTMENT of
INSURANCE
311 West Washington Street # 300
Indianapolis, Indiana 46204-2787
(317) 232-2385
Minimum Limits 25/50/10

IOWA INSURANCE DIVISION
Lucas Bldg. 6th Floor
Des Moines, Iowa 50319
(515) 281-5705
Minimum Limits 20/40/15

KANSAS INSURANCE
DEPARTMENT
420 S/W Ninth Street
Topeka, Kansas 66612-1678
(800) 432-2484 (In State)
(785) 296-3071
(785) 296-2283 (Fax)
Minimum Limits 25/50/10

KENTUCKY DEPARTMENT of
INSURANCE
215 West Main Street
Frankfort, Kentucky 40601
(800) 595-6053 (In State)
(502) 564-3630
(502) 564-1650 (Fax)
Minimum Limits 25/50/10

LOUISIANA DEPARTMENT
of INSURANCE
950 North Fifth Street
Baton Rouge, Louisiana 70804-9214
(800) 259-5300 (In State)
(800) 259-5301 (In State)
(504) 342-5900
Minimum Limits 10/20/10

MAINE BUREAU of
INSURANCE
34 State House Station
Augusta, Maine 04333
(207) 624-8475
(207) 624-8599 (Fax)
Minimum Limits 20/40/10

MARYLAND INSURANCE
ADMININTRATION
501 St.Paul Place 7th Floor
South Baltimore, Maryland 21202-2272
(410) 468-2244
(410) 333-6650 (Fax)
Minimum Limits 20/40/10

MICHIGAN INSURANCE
BUREAU
611 West Ottawa Street 2nd Floor
North
Lansing, Michigan 48933
(517) 373-0220 (Voice)
(517) 335-4978 (Fax)
Minimum Limits 20/40/10

MISSISSIPPI INSURANCE
DEPARTMENT
1804 Walter Sillers Bldg.
Jackson, Mississippi 39201
(800) 562-2957 (In State)
(601) 359-3569
(601) 359-2474 (Fax)
Minimum Limits 10/20/5

MONTANA DEPARTMENT of
INSURANCE
126 North Sanders Rm. 270
Helena, Montana 59620
(406) 444-2040
(406) 444-3497 (Fax)
Minimum Limits 25/50/10

NEVADA DEPARTMENT of
INSURANCE
788 Fairview Drive, Suite 300
Carson City, Nevada 89701
(800) 992-0900 (In State)
(775) 687-4270
(775) 687-3937 (Fax)
Minimum Limits 15/30/10

MASSACHUSETTS DIVISION
of INSURANCE
470 Atlantic Avenue 6th Floor
Boston, Massachusetts 02210-2223
(617) 521-7794
(617) 521-7772
Minimum Limits 20/40/8

MINNESOTA DIVISION of
INSURANCE
85 Seventh Place East, Suite 500
St. Paul, Minnesota 55101
(800) 657-3602 (in state)
(651) 296-2488 (Local)
(651) 296-4328 (Fax)
Minimum Limits 30/60/10

MISSOURI DEPARTMENT of
INSURANCE
P.O. Box 690
Jefferson City, Missouri 65102-0690
(800) 726-7390 (In State)
(573) 751-2640
Minimum Limits 25/50/10

NEBRASKA DEPARTMENT of
INSURANCE
941 'O' Street # 400
Lincoln, Nebraska 68508-3690
(800) 833-0920 (In State)
(402) 471-2201
Minimum Limits 25/50/25

NEW HAMPSHIRE
INSURANCE DEPT.
169 Manchester Street #1
Concord, New Hampshire 03301-5151
(603) 271-2261
Minimum Limits 25/50/25

NEW JERSEY DEPT. of
BANKING INSURANCE
P.O. Box 325
Trenton, New Jersey 08625-0325
(609) 292-5316
(609) 984-5273 (Fax)
Minimum Limits 15/30/5

NEW YORK DEPT. of
INSURANCE
Empire State Plaza, Agency
Bldg. # 1
Albany, New York 12257
(800) 342-3736 (In State)
(518) 474-6600
Minimum Limits 25/50/10
(50/100 for death)

NORTH DAKOTA DEPT. of
INSURANCE
600 East Blvd.
Bismarck, North Dakota 58505-0320
(701) 328-2440
(701) 327-4880 (Fax)
Minimum Limits 25/50/25

OKLAHOMA DEPT. of
INSURANCE
2401 NW 23rd Street, Suite 28
Oklahoma City, Oklahoma 73107
(405) 521-2828
(405) 521-6635 (Fax)
Minimum Limits 10/20/10

PENNSYLVANIA DEPT. of
INSURANCE
1326 Strawberry Square
Harrisburg, Pennsylvania 17120
(717) 787-2317
(717) 783-8585 (Fax)
Minimum Limits 15/30/5

NEW MEXICO INSURANCE
DIVISION
P.O. Drawer 1269
Santa Fe, New Mexico 87504-1269
(505) 827-4601
(505) 827-4734 (Fax)
Minimum Limits 25/50/10

NORTH CAROLINA DEPT. of
INSURANCE
P.O. Box 26387
Raleigh, North Carolina 27611
(800) 546-5664 (In State)
(919) 733-7343
Minimum Limits 30/60/25

OHIO DEPARTMENT of
INSURANCE
2100 Stella Court
Columbus, Ohio 43215-1067
(614) 644-2658
(614) 644-3743
Minimum Limits 12.5/25/7.5

OREGON DEPT. of
COMMERCE & BUSINESS INS.
DIV.
350 Winter Street N.E. Room 200
Salem, Oregon 97310-0200
(503) 947-7980
(503) 378-4351
Minimum Limits 25/50/10

RHODE ISLAND INSURANCE
DEPARTMENT
233 Richmond Street #233
Providence, Rhode Island 02903-4233
(401) 222-2223
(401) 751-4887
Minimum Limits 25/50/25

SOUTH CAROLINA DEPT. of
INSURANCE
P.O. Box 100105
Columbia, South Carolina 29202-3105
(803) 737-6150
(803) 737-6231 (Fax)
Minimum Limits 15/30/5

TENNESSEE DEPT. OF
COMMERCE& INSURANCE
500 James Robertson Pkwy.
Nashville, Tennessee 37243-0565
(615) 741-2176
(615) 741-4000 (Fax)
Minimum Limits 20/50/10

UTAH INSURANCE
DEPARTMENT
3110 State Office Bldg.
Salt Lake City, Utah 84114
(800) 439-3805 (In State)
(801) 538-3800
(801) 538-3829 (Fax)
Minimum Limits 25/50/15

VIRGINIA BUREAU of
INSURANCE
P.O. Box 1157
Richmond, Virginia 23218
(800) 552-7945 (In State)
(804) 371-9741
(804) 371-9873 (Fax)
Minimum Limits 25/50/20

WEST VIRGINIA INSURANCE
DEPT.
P. O. Box 50540
Charleston, West Virginia 25305-0540
(304) 558-3354
(304) 558-0412 (Fax)
Minimum Limits 20/40/10

SOUTH DAKOTA INSURANCE
DIVISION
445 E. Capital Avenue
Pierre, South Dakota 57501
(605) 773-3563
(605) 773-5369 (Fax)
Minimum Limits 25/50/25

TEXAS DEPARTMENT of
INSURANCE
P.O. Box 149104
Austin, Texas 78714-9104
(512) 463-6464
(512) 475-2005 (Fax)
Minimum Limits 20/40/15

VERMONT INSURANCE
DIVISION
89 Main Street - Drawer 20
Montpelier, Vermont 05620-3101
(802) 828-3301
(802) 828-3306
Minimum Limits 20/40/10

WASHINGTON INSURANCE
COMMISSION
P.O. Box 40255
Olympia, Washington 98504-0255
(800) 562-6900 (In State)
(360) 753-7301
(360) 586-3535 (Fax)
Minimum Limits 25/50/10

WISCONSIN INSURANCE
COMMISSION
121 East Wilson Street
Madison, Wisconsin 53702
(800) 236-8517 (In State)
(800) 236-8575 (In State)
(608) 266-3585
(608) 266-9935 (Fax)
Minimum Limits 25/50/10

WYOMING INSURANCE DEPT.
122 West 25th Street, 3rd Floor
East
Cheyenne, Wyoming 82002-0440
(307) 777-7401
Minimum Limits 25/50/20

The Author

Instead of returning to college following service during the Korean War, the writer began what proved to be a life long career in the insurance industry.

Progressing from adjuster, to supervisor to manager and corporate officer, he worked closely in the entire spectrum of claims, claims litigation and public relations.

During the last two decades of his career, he was vice president of an old, highly respected property/casualty company, founded prior to the Civil War. He served on the Loss Managers' committee of the Property Loss Research Bureau, The Insurance Information Institute's Advisory Council on Legal Issues and numerous other industry organizations. He also was a licensed property/casualty insurance agent.

Now retired, he lives in Florida where he has watched with keen interest the many changes that have taken place in the industry.